CREATING
SCULPTED
CAKES

Victoria White

CREATING SCULPTED CAKES

THE CROWOOD PRESS

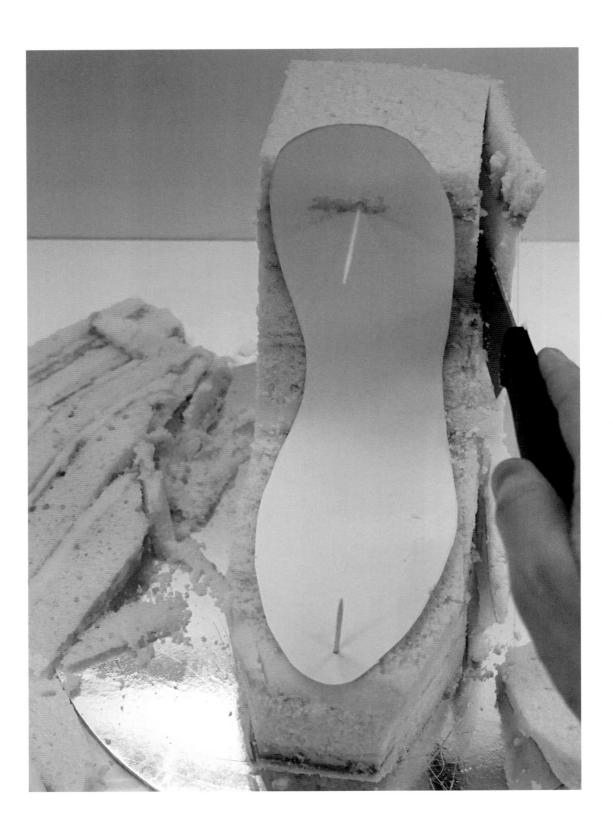

CONTENTS

· · · · · · · ·

	Introduction	7
Chapter 1	Tools and Equipment	11
Chapter 2	Materials	17
Chapter 3	Building Structures	23
Chapter 4	Creating Textures and Basic Shapes	29
Chapter 5	Recipes	33
Chapter 6	Project 1: A Simple Carve	41
Chapter 7	Project 2: Using Templates	51
Chapter 8	Project 3: Carving Vehicles	63
Chapter 9	Project 4: Simple Structure	77
Chapter 10	Project 5: Standing Structure	89
Chapter 11	Project 6: Bust Structure	99
Chapter 12	Project 7: Armature and Airbrushing	111
Chapter 13	Project 8: The Show-Stopper	123
Appendix I	Templates	132
Appendix II	Stockists	140
Appendix III	Conversion Charts	141
	Index	142

INTRODUCTION

· · · · · · · · · · · · · ·

have always had an interest in cake decorating. Baking with my nan is one of my fondest childhood memories. I made my first 'proper' cake for my son's first birthday, following a tutorial in an old cake decorating book. It was a yellow and black fish, and I thought it was marvellous. So I began practising cakes and researching different techniques in books and online and, after many years of practice, decided to enter a competition – and not just any competition, the Cake International. I entered the carved category and made a dragon. I was thrilled to be awarded a bronze, even though my dragon was cross-eyed and only had one leg. I had discovered a love of sculpted cakes that has continued to this day.

Sculpted cakes are always a popular choice for any occasion. The projects in this book are suitable for those looking to start carving cakes, but who don't know where to begin. Have you ever looked at a cake and been completely baffled at how it is standing? If you have questioned how the structure is put together, what materials to use, how to carve the proportions and what covering is best to decorate the cake with, then this is the book for you.

The projects in this book have been designed to teach you the skills and techniques to create head-turning cakes with a realistic finish. The cakes should be made in project order, as each one introduces new techniques that follow on to the next cake. We start with a simple cake shape to help you get familiar with carving, then move on to using templates, sculpting vehicles, adding structure, using the airbrush and finish by putting it all together to make a gravity-defying, show-stopping cake.

The opening chapters will cover the equipment and materials needed to sculpt cakes, starting with

◀ An Easter bulldog cake created for an online cake school.

the basic set of tools I use and a few extras that are helpful for more advanced modelling. I have tried to use similar tools for every project, so you won't need to purchase lots of new tools.

You will find useful information about the different materials that can be used to build structures, and the different coverings such as buttercream, ganache, sugar paste and modelling chocolate.

Towards the back of the book, you will find the templates for the projects. The best way to use a template is to scan it with your phone or computer, enlarge it to the required size and print it out. The template can then be cut out and used to carve a cake or cut the board shape.

The projects in the book are all popular designs that can be recreated exactly by following the step-by-step instructions, or you can adapt the design by adding personal touches. Experiment with changing the breed of dog, for example or the model of the car. Try making your own templates and structure and, most importantly, have fun!

A panda cake covered with modelling chocolate, with internal structure and armature wire to make the bamboo.

A life-sized dinosaur made for Cake International competition in 2022; it won first place.

CHAPTER 1

TOOLS AND EQUIPMENT

· ·

There is a vast array of sugar-craft tools and equipment available on the market, and it is growing all the time. But what exactly do you need to start creating sculpted cakes?

This chapter will cover the basic tools needed for carving cakes and highlight the most useful. Most of these tools are used in every project in the book, so you will not need to keep purchasing more new equipment as you go.

The following tools are a good starting point for all cake-decorating genres. You can then grow your kit with more specialised tools as you progress and advance your skill set.

STAND MIXER

These mixers are attached to a stand and sit on the worktop, with a removable bowl on the base. Different attachments are added for different mixing requirements, and can be used for mixing cake batter, whipping buttercream and making royal icing, among other things. A stand mixer is a great investment for any baker, and they are available in a wide range of colours and designs. Research the different features and choose one to fit your budget. A good-quality mixer will make your baking life easier and last for many years.

BAKING TINS

Invest in good-quality aluminium baking tins. These are lightweight and distribute heat evenly for a great bake every time. I personally like to use PME baking tins with a fixed base. There are a wide variety of shapes and sizes on the market, so try to purchase ones you will use most often to begin with. Round and square tins in 15cm,

◀ Tools and equipment used for creating sculpted cakes.

An array of baking tins. I prefer the fixed bottom tins but spring-base pans are also suitable.

20cm and 25cm sizes are a good starting point, and will not take up too much cupboard space. A rectangular tin is a good option too, as the cake can be cut to create shapes and smaller cakes. In the UK, cake tins are still often sold in inches – *see* the conversion table in Appendix III.

KNIVES

A large serrated knife is essential for carving cakes; a small serrated knife is handy for more delicate carving.

Pallet Knife

A pallet knife is an essential part of your cake craft tool set. They are used for spreading buttercream, fillings and ganache, lifting cakes and small decorations, trimming sugar paste and for buttercream decorating. They come in a wide range of sizes and shapes. I recommend purchasing a 15cm angled blade pallet knife.

Craft Knife

A craft knife or scalpel is used for cutting sugar paste. There are a variety available – some are disposable, and others have replaceable blades. They are not expensive to purchase so experiment with different brands until you find one you are most comfortable using. Craft knives are also used to cut poly-dowels.

SMOOTHERS

Smoothers are another essential part of your kit. Ridged smoothers are used for creating smooth finishes, keeping sides straight and rolling out neat, even ropes of sugar paste. Look for a smoother with a squared back end for smoothing out air bubbles and creating straight angles, and a rounded front to avoid leaving marks in the sugar paste.

The flexi smoother is designed to give your cake a flawless finish. Sharp, clean, sugar paste edges can be achieved as well as smooth ganache. These smoothers usually come in a set of different sizes and shapes and can vary in thickness. My favourite is the sugar smoother set from Sugarworks.

ROLLING PINS

Rolling pins come in various lengths and weights for different jobs. They can be smooth for rolling out sugar paste or embossed with a pattern. A small and a large rolling pin in your kit should cover all bases.

MODELLING TOOLS

You can purchase a basic modelling tool kit from almost all sugar-craft suppliers. This will include a shell and blade tool used for embossing and trimming sugar paste, a bone tool for frilling and smoothing petals and leaves, a ball tool for making round indentations and curves and a scallop and comb tool for cutting scalloped edges and embossing mouths on modelled figures.

The tool used most often by cake decorators is the double-ended Dresden tool. It has a narrow point at one end and a spooned tip at the other. It can be used for a variety of techniques including texturing, marking details, making creases and facial features, smoothing and sculpting.

Modelling tools come in different materials, in packs or sold individually. I prefer metal tools as they have no seams, are weightier and better quality. They can be expensive but last longer than plastic tools, which tend to snap.

Silicone Modelling Tools

The tools I would not be without are my sugar shapers by Sugarworks. These silicone tools have a variety of different tips that are perfect for sculpting. The sides of the tools can be used to smooth and blend modelling chocolate.

Silicone-tipped tools are also very useful. They come in various sizes, and are hard- or soft-tipped.

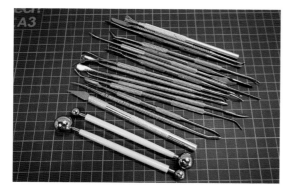

There is a wide variety of modelling tools available on the market. Begin with the basics and grow your kit collection as your skills progress.

My favourite tools to use for sculpting are sugar shapers.

They are used for adding details and drawing soft lines.

Stitching Tool

A stitching tool is rolled along the paste to leave small lines that look like stitches, and is used to give a realistic finish when sculpting fabrics.

Wire Rake Tool

The rake tool is a metal tool with wire prongs like a rake. It is used to create fur and hair textures.

CUTTERS AND PLUNGER CUTTERS

Cutters are used to cut shapes from sugar paste, and are plastic or metal. Plunger cutters have a push-down plunger on the end, which is usually embossed to add pattern to the shape. As a starting point, I recommend a set of circle and square cutters and some plunger cutters with basic shapes such as circles, stars, hearts and flowers. Alphabet and number plunger cutters are also extremely useful.

PAINTBRUSHES

A selection of paintbrushes in various sizes is a must for any cake decorator. Choose good-quality brushes and clean them after every use with dish soap.

Fine brushes are used for painting details such as eyes, whereas thicker brushes are useful for larger areas. Always check the brushes for loose fibres and chipping paint before use.

CORNFLOUR POUCH

If you are having trouble with sugar paste or modelling chocolate sticking to the work surface or your hands, apply a light dusting of cornflour to help prevent this. A cornflour pouch is a fine mesh bag that holds the cornflour. I like to use the Wilton Dust-N-Store pouch as it has a container, but you can make your own dusting pouch very simply.

Making a Dusting Pouch

To make a dusting pouch for cornflour, take a new, washed, pair of tights and cut off the foot sections. Stretch one of the legs over a glass to make it easier to fill and spoon some cornflour inside. Remove it from the glass and tie the end, close to the cornflour.

You could also use a piece of muslin or cheesecloth by placing some cornflour in the centre and gathering up the sides, securing them with an elastic band.

Making a cornflour pouch from a pair of stockings.

A selection of paintbrushes.

SCISSORS

A small pair of scissors is useful for cutting dowels and templates, and creating texture in sugar paste.

TAPE MEASURE AND RULER

A tape measure is essential for measuring cakes and decorations. A ruler can also be used to take measurements and to help cut straight lines; a metal one is best so it can't be accidently cut with a craft knife.

AIRBRUSH

An airbrush is used to colour cakes quickly and easily, creating depth and a professional-looking finish. Many colours are available with different finishes, such as pearl or matt, and can be mixed to create your own shades.

Airbrushes come with a compressor and hose, or as a portable version with a battery unit attached to the pen. Airbrushing techniques are covered in Chapter 2.

STEAMER

Steam is used to remove cornflour and icing sugar from sugar paste, and to set dust colours to prevent smudging and colour transfer. It can also be used to create a glossy finish. You can purchase a dedicated cake steamer, or a hand-held clothes steamer will work just as well.

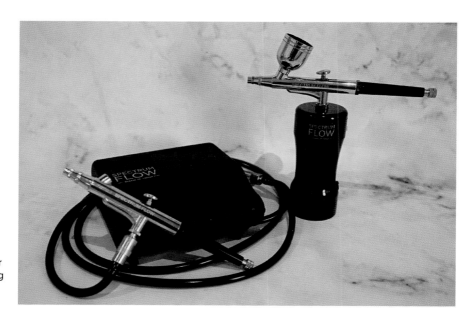

An airbrush is used for colouring and creating realistic paint effects on sculpted cakes.

CHAPTER 2

MATERIALS

· · · · · · · · · ·

This chapter looks at the materials available for sculpting cakes. Sugar paste and modelling chocolate are widely used for both covering cakes and sculpting detail. Both can be coloured, painted and airbrushed, so how do you choose which to use and when?

SUGAR PASTE

Sugar paste is also known as fondant or ready-to-roll icing. It is used for covering cakes and drums, and making modelled elements and decorations. It can be used with moulds and cutters, and sets firm. Sugar paste most commonly comes in white but is also available in an array of colours. It can be smoothed and polished, giving a professional finish to cakes.

The advantage of sugar paste is that it is available to purchase in almost all local supermarkets

Sugar paste can be bought in various colours.

as well as in sugar-craft shops. Try out different brands to see which you prefer; they can vary in elasticity and softness.

The main disadvantage of sugar paste is that once it has dried, you can't rework it. If you are working on a large cake that may take several days, sugar paste is not the best option. It can also be difficult to blend and can tear when adding textures.

◀ Materials used for sculpting cakes.

MODELLING CHOCOLATE

Modelling chocolate is a favourite among cake sculptors. It is extremely easy to blend and sculpt with and create fine details. Modelling chocolate is made by adding syrup to melted chocolate, creating a firm but malleable paste that holds its own shape. It is not as widely available in shops as sugar paste (it's mainly bought from online suppliers) but you can make your own quite easily (*see* Chapter 5).

Modelling chocolate softens as it warms, so if you have particularly hot hands, it may be difficult to work with. The advantage of it is that it doesn't dry out like sugar paste, so you can keep working on your project for several days. It can be used in moulds and can be coloured with gel colour. I prefer to work with white modelling chocolate so it can be coloured, but dark versions are also available.

Sculpting chocolate is commercially available and contains more sugar than cocoa butter, making it firmer than modelling chocolate. It is great for making models but can be expensive if you need a large amount.

GANACHE

Ganache is a mixture of melted chocolate and cream used to crumb coat and cover cakes to create a smooth base. Ganache is firm once set, so several layers can be applied to add stability to structured cakes.

There are three main types of ganache: dark chocolate, white chocolate and milk chocolate. Different ratios of chocolate to cream are used for each type (*see* Chapter 5). Ganache can be used for a filling, a frosting or as a drip, or to make truffles. It can also be coloured and flavoured with the likes of orange, mint or rum.

Ganache is used as a crumb coat (a thin layer of icing used to cover cakes to hold the crumbs in place) and to add stability to cakes.

RICE KRISPIE TREATS (RKT)

RKT is rice cereal combined with melted marshmallows to create a lightweight yet firm substitute for cake where strength and stability are needed. It can be shaped and modelled when it is warm, but once cooled, it sets solid. RKT is perfect for using on sculpted cakes to make an awkward-shaped head, for example. It can be covered with ganache and sugar paste/modelling chocolate and can also be carved in its solid state.

Rice Krispie treats used to create a circus ball in Project 8.

COLOURING: GELS, DUSTS AND AIRBRUSHING

Gel Colours

Gel pastes are ideal for colouring sugar paste, buttercream, marzipan, modelling chocolate, royal icing and cake batter. The gel is highly concentrated, meaning you only need a small amount to achieve the desired colour. Adding lots of colour can change the consistency of sugar paste and modelling chocolate, making it sticky and difficult to work with, so a high-concentration colour is advantageous.

For black and red, it's advisable to purchase pre-mixed black and red sugar pastes. These strong colours are difficult to achieve without changing the consistency of the sugar paste.

The same colouring technique can be used for modelling chocolate, but you may need to rest the chocolate in the refrigerator if it gets too warm when kneading.

Pre-coloured sugar pastes can be mixed to make new colours. Adding black can darken the colour, while adding white can lighten it. Using pre-coloured sugar pastes to make darker colours is beneficial as it saves having to add more colour gel, changing the consistency of the paste.

A selection of gel colours.

Sugar pastes are available in many different colours and can be mixed to create new shades.

Colouring Sugar Paste with Gel Colours

Wearing gloves, add a small drop of gel colour to the white sugar paste and fold it in. Knead the sugar paste until you achieve a uniform colour. It is better to start with a small amount of colour and add more to create a stronger shade, than to try and lighten it with more white paste. Once you have achieved the desired shade, wrap the sugar paste in clingfilm and leave it to rest. The colour will darken slightly.

Dust Colours

Dust colours are edible powders used for adding colour and shading to cakes and models. They can be used dry, straight out of the pot or mixed with liquid such as alcohol or dipping solution to make a paint. Dusts come in a huge array of colours and

Dust colours come in an array of colours and finishes.

finishes. Lustre and metallic dusts give a shimmer effect and twinkle dust creates a sparkly finish.

Dipping Solution

Dipping solution is a food-grade ethanol used in sugar craft. It is used to colour sugar paste and create food-safe paint. Any type of colouring can be added to the solution, before dipping the sugar paste in it to leave a glossy, vibrant finish. It is particularly good for colouring petals and cake toppers.

Dipping solution can also be used to make a paint by mixing it with dust colours. Pour a little into a small pot and add a pinch of colour dust. Mix to dissolve the dust and the paint is ready to use. When the alcohol has evaporated, the dust is left behind and will need to be sealed with a steamer.

Using the Airbrush

Airbrushing your cakes allows you to create realistic effects, blending colours and creating gradients not achievable with other colouring methods.

There are a few factors to remember when using the airbrush. Keep the angle of the pen at 45 degrees when spraying the whole cake. For sharper lines and details, spray at a 90-degree angle. Keep the airbrush 15–20cm away from your cake and try to maintain an even pressure. Pull the trigger halfway back until the colour flows and keep it steady to avoid patches.

A large cardboard box makes a perfect spraying booth to protect your surfaces from overspray. If you do not have a box to hand, cover the area in newspaper or plastic. Place the cake on a turntable in the centre of the spray area to make turning it easier.

Put a few drops of colour into the fluid cup; a little goes a long way, so don't overfill. Gently pull the trigger back for a steady flow of colour and begin spraying in a back and forth motion, moving from the elbow. Remember to maintain a consistent distance from the cake to achieve an even coat. Apply the lightest shades first, building layers of colour to create depth and shadows, letting each layer dry before spraying the next coat.

Practise drawing fine lines, shading and drawing loops. Try writing with the airbrush and experiment with using stencils.

Mixing dipping solution with dust colours to create an edible paint.

Airbrush colours are available in many colours and finishes.

Clean the airbrush thoroughly afterwards to avoid clogging and ensure that it is ready for the next use.

Airbrush Colours

Airbrush colours are either water-based or ethanol-based, and come in a wide range of colours and finishes. Water-based colours can be mixed easily and are not as expensive as the ethanol-based ones, but they cannot be used on chocolate. They take longer to dry, and the colours tend to mix when painting layers. The ethanol-based colours are a little more expensive but can be used on all media can be layered and blended, and dry almost immediately.

OTHER MATERIALS

Edible Glue

Edible glue is used to stick sugar paste or modelling chocolate together. Water can be used for small pieces, but if strength is needed – for attaching arms to a cake, for example – edible glue is more suitable. It is widely available online and in stores, but it can also be made at home by adding a pinch of Tylose powder to a small jar of water.

Tylose or CMC Powder

Tylose powder is a hardening agent that can be added to fondant, creating a modelling paste that sets hard. It is also used to make edible glue.

Confectioner's Glaze

Confectioner's glaze is applied to sugar paste or modelling chocolate to create a shiny finish. It is particularly good for painting on eyes and on teeth to give them a realistic shine. It comes in a small bottle and is applied with a paintbrush, which will need cleaning with special glaze cleaner after use. Confectioner's glaze is also available as an aerosol spray, which is useful for larger areas, such as on a car.

CHAPTER 3

BUILDING STRUCTURES

· ·

With a well-planned internal structure, you can create impressive, gravity-defying cakes. You can buy cake structure frames and sets from suppliers such as Zoe's Fancy Cakes and Dinkydoodle, or you can make your own to suit your cake's design.

EQUIPMENT

Cake Boards

The baseboard for the cake needs to be strong to support the structure. For small cakes with a simple dowelled structure, a regular cake drum can be used. For larger cakes, with multiple platforms and cake boards, it is best to use MDF board. MDF can be cut to any shape and size and comes in a variety of thicknesses. Pre-cut, food-safe MDF round cake drums are available to purchase from Prop Options.

Internal Supports

Dowels

Dowel rods can be made of either wood or plastic. Wooden dowels can be sharpened to pierce cake boards when centre dowelling. Plastic dowels come in various diameters and lengths, and offer greater support, so fewer are needed.

Threaded Rods

The most common internal structures are made from steel threaded rods or PVC pipe. I prefer to use threaded rods as they are strong and readily available from local hardware stores and online. Rods can also be bent to shape and are easily attached to boards with washers and nuts. They

◀ Structures are used to create gravity-defying, show-stopping cakes.

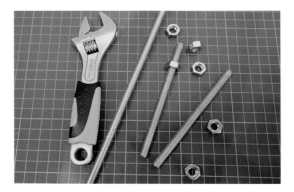

Threaded rods are used to make structure. They come in various diameters and lengths.

are available in various thicknesses and lengths, and can easily be cut to size using a jeweller's or hacksaw.

PVC Pipe

PVC is often used for internal structure as it is easy to fit together and widely available in various lengths and thicknesses that can be cut to size. Different fittings can be attached to create joints and the pipe can be gently heated and bent. A plumbing flange is needed to attach the pipe to the board with wood screws.

Armature Wire

Armature wire is used in sculpting and other crafts. It is a pliable wire that can be twisted and shaped to make supports for small, delicate areas, such as fairy wings or an elephant's trunk. Armature wire comes in a variety of gauges and can be cut to size with wire cutters. It is incredibly useful in modelling and can be bought from craft stores and online.

Other Equipment

To build the structure, you will need a drill to make holes in the boards for rods or dowels, or a screwdriver and wood screws to attach the flange if using PVC pipe. You will also need a saw to cut boards and rods. A clamp or vice is useful to hold the material in place while cutting.

Furniture pads are sticky foam pads that can be attached to the underside of the baseboard to lift it from the surface. This allows space for the nuts and washers and make it easier to move a heavy cake around. You can make your own pads using foam board or small blocks of wood attached with hot glue.

Aluminium foil tape is a roll of self-adhesive foil that is used to make the structure food safe. No metal can come into contact with the cake.

A hot-glue gun is also useful for securing dowels and wire.

Armature wire used for supporting finer sections, such as the elephant's trunk in Project 8.

Other equipment used for carving cakes. From left to right: screwdriver, adjustable spanner, aluminium foil tape, drill, clamp, hacksaw.

DESIGNING THE INTERNAL STRUCTURE

The first step in designing internal structure is drawing a template. Even if you do not intend on using a template to carve the cake, it is essential to determine where the support will be needed. Sketch out your cake design to the correct size and draw in a line for the baseboard. Next, determine where the cake will need supports and decide the best materials to use. Draw the platforms on the template, remembering the thickness of the boards, and then add the rods/pipes. Once you have the structure planned out, you can take the measurements of

The astronaut cake template.
Print at 29cm tall.

Tightening the nuts on the underside with an adjustable spanner.

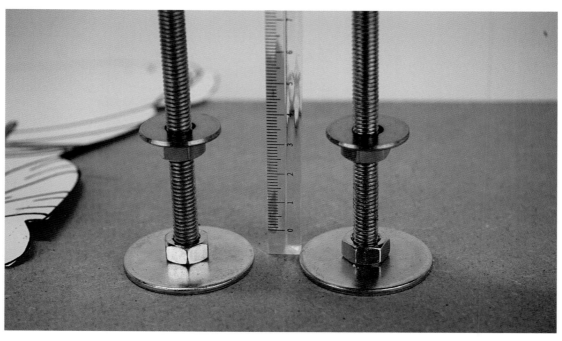
Measuring the placement of the nuts and washers for the lower platform.

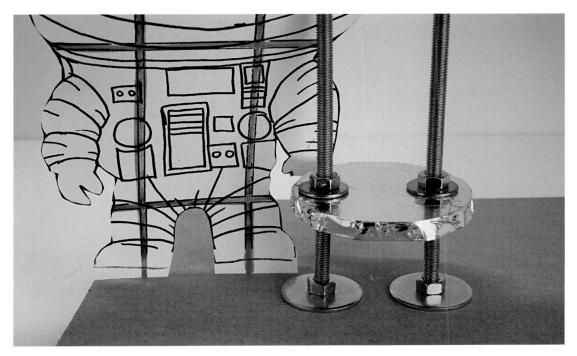

Position the lower platform and secure it with washers and nuts, ensuring it is level.

all the elements and begin building. The astronaut template is shown here as an example.

Place the template on the board in the required position and mark the placement of the rods. With an 8mm drill bit, drill the two holes for the rods into the baseboard. Use these holes as a template to drill the 8cm and 12cm round board holes, making sure they are central and the three boards line up. To make the round boards food safe, cover both sides with aluminium foil tape. Flip the baseboard over and stick on foam furniture feet pads in each of the corners.

Place the threaded rod through the hole in the baseboard, adding a washer then a nut to the bottom of the rod. Thread a washer and nut on the top of the rod and finger tighten the nut while holding the one underneath still. Tighten the nuts with an adjustable spanner so the rod is completely secure. Repeat on the other side. Using the template, measure where the first platform sits, and add nuts and washers to the rods. Push the 8cm board onto the rods and add the top washers and nuts. Tighten with the spanner, making sure the board is level.

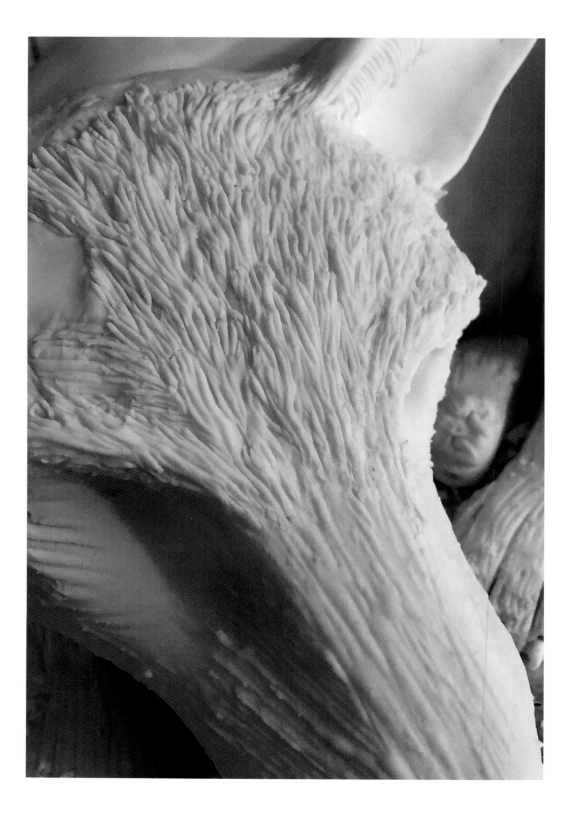

CHAPTER 4

CREATING TEXTURES AND BASIC SHAPES

· · · · · · · · · · · · ·

Adding texture to cakes can enhance the design and create realistic results. There are many ways to create texture, using store-bought tools or everyday items. Experiment with different items to make different textures – you are not limited to your sugar-craft kit.

TEXTURES

Impression Mats Impression mats are silicone or plastic mats used to emboss texture onto sugar paste. They are available in a variety of patterns such as bark, bricks, scales and the knitting mat used in Project 6 in this book. An impression mat can be used in two ways – before or after the sugar paste is on the cake. For the first method, roll out the sugar paste on the work surface to the required size and dust the mat with cornflour. Push the impression mat into the sugar paste using even pressure to emboss the pattern, then apply the paste onto the cake. This technique is good for round and square cakes. The second way is to emboss the sugar paste or modelling chocolate directly on the cake. This works well for shaped cakes and for textures such as fur, where a variety of depths is needed.

Modelling Tools Modelling tools can be used to create texture such as hair, fur, leather and scales.

Creating fur texture with a Dresden tool.

◀ Textures can give a cake a realistic finish and can be made with specialised tools or everyday household objects.

Use the Dresden or silicone tool to create fur by drawing long and short wavy lines in the paste, varying the depth to intensify the effect. Hair can be made in the same way with longer strokes. A leathery look, such as elephant skin, can be created with light strokes of the silicone tool in an X shape.

Specialised texturing tools are also available; have a look online at clay sculpture supply retailers and in stage make-up shops. Skin texturising tools are used to create fine pores, and a raking tool can be used to create light fur or hair texture.

Aluminium Foil Foil is fantastic for creating textures such as concrete, wood, cracks and leather. Screw up a piece of foil and push it into the paste to create a deep, cracked look or flatten out the screwed-up foil for a lighter texture.

Plastic or Paper Straws Straws are perfect for making scales on a dinosaur or fish, for example. Squeeze the tip of the straw into a misshapen circle, and lightly push it into the paste. Turn the straw each time so the scales are different and reshape the end every so often to create a variety of shape. Using different-size straws can create a realistic effect.

Sponges Sponges can be used to create a variety of textures on paste and with food colour paint. A new scouring pad can create grass, fur or even skin texture. An array of stage make-up sponges are useful as they come in varying degrees of coarseness. These can be used to stipple paint as well as for textures.

Toothbrushes A brand-new toothbrush can create interesting effects on paste, such as grass, fur or fabric. Push the bristles into the paste, varying the pressure to create different effects.

Mesh or Netting A wire mesh can be used to create a diamond pattern on the paste, which could be useful for scales and fabrics. Netting can be embossed by laying it over the paste and running over it with a smoother to leave a light texture.

MODELLING BASIC SHAPES

Creating realistic carved cakes involves a degree of modelling for details such as limbs, hands and facial features. Almost all basic modelling shapes start with a ball.

Scales can be made with the end of a drinking straw.

Balls Roll a piece of sugar paste or modelling chocolate between the palms of your hands to create the ball shape. If you find the ball has cracks or creases, gently push your palms together to slightly flatten the ball as you roll, which will bring the paste together. Roll the ball in your hands until it is smooth and spherical in shape. Ball shapes can be used as eyes, heads and noses in cartoon-style models.

Teardrops and Cones Roll a ball shape in your hands. Bring your palms together on one side to form a V shape and gently roll the ball back and forth to taper it on one side. You can also create a teardrop shape with you finger and thumb if it is very small, for example to make the dragon's claws in Project 7. To create a cone, make a teardrop shape but flatten off the thicker end.

Discs A disc is created by rolling a ball, then flattening it to make a flat circle. This technique is used to make the cobblestones for Project 7. It can be useful if you don't have the correct-sized circle cutter.

Cubes Begin with a ball shape and flatten the opposite sides between two smoothers, or your fingers if it is small. Turn the shape and repeat until you have a cube shape. It can be tricky to get straight sides. Another way to create a cube is to slice the edges with a sharp knife.

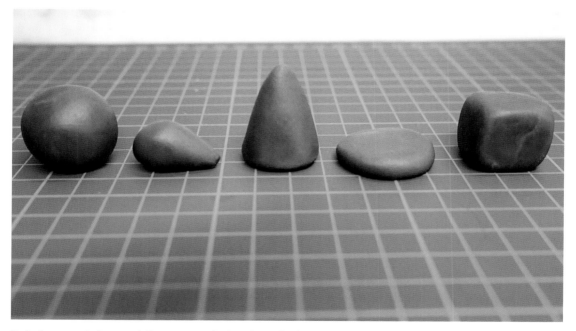

Basic shapes made from modelling paste are the foundation for all sculptures.

CHAPTER 5

RECEIPES

· · · · ·

n this section you will find all the recipes used for the projects in this book. I have included two types of cake, a vanilla sponge and a madeira cake. I use the vanilla sponge recipe for all the project cakes, but you may prefer to make madeira cake. Madeira is denser than the sponge cake as it contains plain flour as well as self-raising. This means it holds shape well and is easy to carve. Try both and see which you prefer.

BASIC VANILLA SPONGE

This is the recipe I use for most of my cakes. It is soft and light but strong enough to be carved into simple shapes. The sponge can be flavoured with cocoa powder or other flavourings, and it can be used for cupcakes and traybakes.

The cake batter is divided into two tins, each making a cake 6cm deep. These cakes can then

Ingredients

Round tin size	15cm	18cm	20cm	23cm	25cm	28cm	30cm	33cm
Square tin size	13cm	15cm	18cm	20cm	23cm	25cm	28cm	30cm
Margarine	300g	400g	500g	600g	750g	900g	1.1kg	1.3kg
Caster sugar	300g	400g	500g	600g	750g	900g	1.1kg	1.3kg
Self-raising flour	300g	400g	500g	600g	750g	900g	1.1kg	1.3kg
Eggs	6	8	10	12	15	18	22	25
Vanilla extract	½ tsp	¾ tsp	1 tsp	1¼ tsp	1½ tsp	1¾ tsp	2 tsp	2¼ tsp
Baking time	50 min	55 min	1 hr	1 hr 10 min	1 hr 15 min	1 hr 20 min	1 hr 30 min	1 hr 40 min

◀ Ingredients for making the basic vanilla sponge.

be split in half to make the 3cm layers used in the projects.

Method

1. Preheat the oven to 180°C/160°C fan/350°F/ gas mark 4.
2. Line the base and sides of both tins with greaseproof paper.
3. Whisk together the margarine and caster sugar with a paddle attachment on an electric mixer to incorporate air, so it is lighter in colour and fluffy. Scrape down the sides and base of bowl to release any stuck margarine.
4. Beat the eggs and gradually add them to the mixing bowl with the sugar and margarine. If using ten eggs or more, add a spoon of the flour as you incorporate the eggs to prevent the mixture from splitting. If it does split, it will come back together as you add more flour. Split batter does not affect the taste of the cake, but the texture may be more dense, as the fat is not dispersed evenly.
5. Add the vanilla extract. If you are making a flavoured cake, add the flavouring now.
6. Add the self-raising flour to the bowl and mix slowly until it is just combined. Remove the bowl from the mixer and scrape down the sides and base to ensure all the flour is incorporated. Do not overmix the batter or the air may be knocked out, resulting in a poor rise.
7. Divide the mixture between the two prepared baking tins.
8. Bake in the centre of the oven for the stated time. Do not be tempted to open the oven door to check progress until the end of the time.
9. Remove the cake from the oven using oven gloves. The cake should be golden and firm to the touch. Test if it is ready by inserting a skewer or sharp knife. The skewer should come out clean, indicating the cake is cooked inside. If there is still mixture on the skewer, return the cake to the oven for a few minutes before checking again.
10. Leave the cake to cool in the tin for around 10 minutes, then turn it out onto a cool rack. Carefully remove the greaseproof paper if it has stuck to the cake.
11. Allow the cake to cool completely before splitting and filling. If you are not using the cake straight away, wrap it tightly in clingfilm and place it in the fridge or freezer until it is needed.

Layers of vanilla sponge, held together with vanilla buttercream.

MADEIRA CAKE

Ingredients

Round tin size	15cm	18cm	20cm	23cm	25cm	28cm	30cm	33cm
Square tin size	13cm	15cm	18cm	20cm	23cm	25cm	28cm	30cm
Margarine	175g	225g	350g	450g	550g	700g	850g	1kg
Caster sugar	175g	225g	350g	450g	550g	700g	850g	1kg
Self-raising flour	175g	225g	350g	450g	550g	700g	850g	1kg
Plain flour	75g	125g	175g	225g	275g	350g	425g	500g
Eggs	3	4	6	8	10	12	15	18
Vanilla extract	½ tsp	¾ tsp	1 tsp	1¼ tsp	1½ tsp	1¾ tsp	2 tsp	2¼ tsp
Baking time	1 hr	1 hr	1 hr 15 min	1 hr30 min	1 hr 30 min	1 hr 45 min	2 hr	2 hr 15 min

Method

1. Preheat the oven to 180°C/160°C fan/350°F/ gas mark 4.
2. Line the base and sides of both tins with greaseproof paper.
3. Whisk together the margarine and caster sugar with a paddle attachment on an electric mixer to incorporate air, so it is lighter in colour and fluffy. Scrape down the sides and base of bowl to release any stuck margarine.
4. Beat the eggs and gradually add them to the mixing bowl with the sugar and margarine. If using ten eggs or more, add a spoon of the flour as you incorporate the eggs to prevent the mixture splitting. If it does split, it will come back together as you add more flour. Split batter does not affect the taste of the cake, but the texture may be more dense, as the fat is not dispersed evenly.
5. Add the vanilla extract. If you are making a flavoured cake, add the flavouring now.
6. Add the self-raising flour and plain flour to the bowl and mix slowly until it is just combined. Remove the bowl from the mixer and scrape down the sides and base to ensure all the flour is incorporated. Do not overmix the batter or the air may be knocked out, resulting in a poor rise.
7. Divide the mixture between the two prepared baking tins.
8. Bake in the centre of the oven for the stated time. Do not be tempted to open the oven door to check the progress until the end of the time.
9. Remove the cake from the oven using oven gloves. The cake should be golden and firm to the touch. Test if it is ready by inserting a skewer or sharp knife. The skewer should come

Pouring the batter into the cake tin.

out clean, indicating the cake is cooked inside. If there is still mixture on the skewer, return the cake to the oven for a few minutes before checking again.

10. Leave the cake to cool in the tin for around 10 minutes, then turn it out onto a cool rack. Carefully remove the greaseproof paper if it has stuck to the cake.

11. Allow the cake to cool completely before splitting and filling. If you are not using the cake straight away, wrap it tightly in clingfilm and place it in the fridge or freezer until it is needed.

Whipping the buttercream, so it is light and fluffy.

3. Add the vanilla extract and turn the mixer up to medium and beat the buttercream for a further 5 minutes. It should be pale in colour, smooth and silky.

AMERICAN BUTTERCREAM – VANILLA

This recipe makes one batch of buttercream. The vanilla extract can be substituted for other flavourings. American buttercream is the best type of buttercream to use with carved cakes as it sets firm with a crust, helping with the stability of the cake. It can be used for filling the cake and for the crumb coat.

Ingredients

250g salted butter (or unsalted, if preferred)
500g icing sugar
¼ tsp vanilla extract

Method

1. Place the butter in the mixing bowl and beat with an electric mixer for 5–10 minutes until it is light and soft.

2. With the mixer on the lowest setting, gradually add the icing sugar until it is all incorporated, to prevent creating a dust cloud.

GANACHE

There are three types of chocolate ganache: white, milk and dark. Each uses a different ratio of chocolate to cream. Below is the recipe to make one batch of ganache as used in the projects in the book. Ganache is mainly used as a crumb coat as it sets firm, adding stability to the cake. It can also be whipped and used as a filling, melted and used as a drip or chilled to make truffles.

Any variety of chocolate is suitable for making ganache. Supermarket own-brand chocolate slabs keep the cost down, or you can use branded

	Ratio of chocolate:cream	Double cream	Chocolate
White chocolate	3:1	300g	900g
Milk chocolate	3:1	300g	900g
Dark chocolate	2:1	300g	600g

chocolate nibs, chips or candy melts. Try a few different brands and see what works for you.

Method

The easiest way to make ganache is with the microwave.

1. Break the chocolate into small pieces and place them into a microwaveable bowl.
2. Melt the chocolate in bursts of 30 seconds on full power, stirring well in between bursts, until the chocolate has all melted and there are no lumps. Be very careful not to overheat the chocolate, as it will burn.
3. Pour the cream into a microwaveable jug and heat for 1 minute.
4. Pour the hot cream into the melted chocolate and stir until it the mixture is glossy and smooth and comes away from the sides of the bowl.
5. Cover the ganache in a sheet of clingfilm, pushing the clingfilm down until it touches the surface of the ganache. This is to ensure a crust does not form.
6. Leave the ganache to cool at room temperature or in the refrigerator. It is ready to use when it is at peanut butter consistency.

If the ganache sets too hard, it can be warmed very briefly in the microwave to melt it slightly. If it is overheated it may split, which is when the oils separate from the chocolate. If this happens, add a teaspoon of cooled boiled water and stir until it comes back together. This may take some time!

Ganache can also be made on the hob by heating the cream in a saucepan until it just starts to boil. Pour the cream over the broken-up chocolate and leave to stand for 2 minutes. Stir the cream into the chocolate, which should now be melted, until the mixture comes away from the sides of the bowl. If the chocolate is not quite melted, heat the ganache in the saucepan over a low heat, stirring thoroughly until it is smooth.

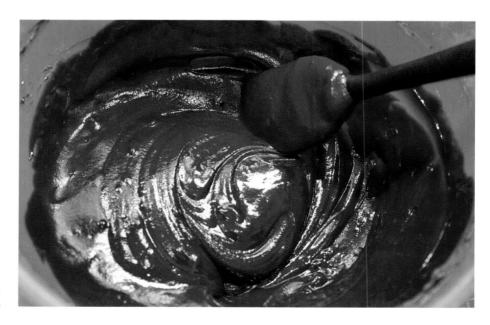

Adding cream to melted chocolate to make ganache.

MODELLING CHOCOLATE

Modelling chocolate is a cake sculptor's best friend. It's fairly expensive to buy yet can be made at home with just two ingredients, though it is a little tricky. I like to use white chocolate, as it can be easily coloured and painted.

Melting white chocolate to make modelling chocolate.

Ingredients

450g white chocolate
250g golden syrup

Method

1. Place the white chocolate in a microwaveable bowl and melt it in 30-second bursts on full power, stirring between each burst, until the chocolate is melted and smooth.
2. Pour the golden syrup into a jug and heat it in the microwave for 10 seconds. Golden syrup heats up very quickly so don't leave it in too long.

Adding golden syrup to the melted chocolate.

3. Pour the warmed golden syrup over the melted chocolate and fold them together with a spatula, until the chocolate becomes thick and starts to pull away from the sides of the bowl. This happens quite quickly, so try to incorporate all of the syrup. Do not overmix, as the oils will start to separate from the chocolate.
4. Lay out some clingfilm on the work surface and pour the mixture on. Place another sheet of clingfilm over the top and press the chocolate into a flat disc, around 1cm thick. Wrap the edges and place the chocolate in the fridge for 30 minutes.

Modelling chocolate.

5. Remove the chocolate from the fridge and leave it to rest at room temperature overnight.

6. Unwrap the modelling chocolate and knead it until it is soft and pliable. If the chocolate is too hard to knead, place it in the microwave for 5 seconds at a time to warm it slightly.

Troubleshooting

If your modelling chocolate is too greasy after kneading it, allow it to rest on a sheet for 10–20 minutes. Knead it on a cold surface to cool it quickly and bring the oil back into the chocolate. A metal cookie sheet that has been cooled in the fridge works well, but make sure it is completely dry. Water and modelling chocolate do not mix!

If your chocolate is dry and crumbly, you can add more syrup, a tablespoon at a time. Keep kneading until it is smooth and pliable.

Combining crisped rice cereal and marshmallows to make RKT.

RICE KRISPIE TREATS – RKT

Rice Krispie treats are an easy and fun way to add details to sculpted cakes. They are a great alternative to cake where strength and stability is needed.

Ingredients

50g butter
200g marshmallows
150g crisped rice cereal

Method

1. Melt the butter in a saucepan over a low heat and add the marshmallows. The butter stops the marshmallows sticking to the pan.

2. Melt the marshmallows, stirring constantly until they are smooth. Add the rice cereal and mix with a wooden spoon until the cereal is coated with the marshmallow. It will be very hot and very sticky.

3. Once the RKT has cooled enough to handle, tip it out onto some greaseproof paper.

4. Grease your hands with vegetable fat or butter and shape the RKT, squeezing it firmly into the required shape.

5. Place it in the refrigerator to cool. It will set solid and can be carved with a small, serrated knife.

6. RKT can also be turned out into a tin or bowl to create a cube or sphere shape.

> Please note that the numbers on the images in the following chapters are intended to make clear the sequence of images, and do not necessarily correlate directly with the numbers of the steps in the text.

CHAPTER 6

PROJECT 1: A SIMPLE CARVE

· ·

have chosen a backpack cake as the first project, as it is a simple shape, perfect for introducing carving techniques. The design is very versatile and could be adapted for a variety of occasions or themes. It could be a hiking backpack, a school bag, a sports bag in team colours – or add ballet shoes and make it a dance bag. The design we are making in this project is an elegant bag, perfect for a birthday. The backpack cake is placed on a 30cm cake drum, edged with ivory ribbon.

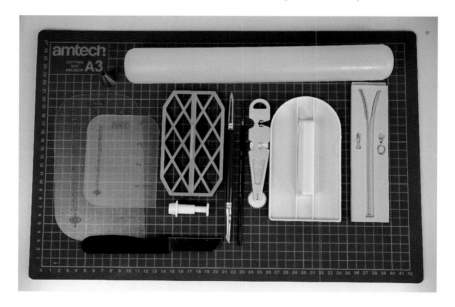

The tools needed for the project.

◀ Project 1: Backpack.

Tools and Materials

Tools

- 30cm cake drum
- Offset pallet knife
- Smoother
- Flexi smoother
- Stitching tool
- Zip mould (Katy Sue 6in zip silicone mould, www.katysuedesigns.com)
- Craft knife/scalpel
- Serrated knife
- Rolling pin
- Ruler
- 2 small paintbrushes
- Small ball tool
- Dresden tool or silicone-tipped tool
- 15mm ivory ribbon
- Double-sided tape or non-toxic glue

Materials

- Cake (*see* Chapter 5): 10cm × 18cm, 7 layers
- Buttercream, 2 batches
- 2kg ivory sugar paste
- 100g black sugar paste
- 800g white sugar paste
- 500g white modelling paste
- Silver lustre dust
- Rejuvenator spirit or vodka
- Cornflour for dusting

METHOD

Carving the Bag Shape

The shape of the backpack is quite simple and sturdy so you will not need to add any extra supports.

1. Start by stacking seven layers of cake, filling each layer with buttercream (you could add jam if desired, though use it sparingly if you do, as too much can make the cake slide).

2. Chill the cake in the freezer (or fridge) until firm to make it easier to carve.

3. Starting approximately 4cm back from the front edge, hold your large, serrated knife at a 45-degree angle and down the front side of the cake to the third layer to create the front of the bag. The offcut should look like a wide triangle.

4. Carve the sides of the top of the cake. Again starting 4cm back from the edge, cut the corners off the cake down to the third layer, to create a flat triangle shape. Leave the back of the cake straight.

5. On each corner from the top of the cake, carve out a triangle shape to create the folds of the bag. These should start at around 2.5cm in thickness from the top, thinning out towards the bottom.

6. Round off all the cut edges to give a softer, more natural look to the bag, including the bottom edge.

7. Cover the whole cake with a layer of buttercream. This traps the crumbs and gives the sugar paste something to stick to, and is known as a crumb coat.

8. Smooth out the crumb coat using a flexi smoother. If the buttercream drags, dip the flexi smoother in hot water to warm it up. You are aiming for a nice, smooth base with no dips or air holes, as these will show up once the sugar paste is applied. Chill the cake for around 15 minutes until the buttercream is firm.

Layers of sponge cake filled with buttercream, stacked and chilled, ready to begin carving.

Carving the slanted front of the bag. Take a little off at a time if you prefer – you can always cut more.

Removing the top corners to make a flat triangle shape.

Carving out tapered triangles on each of the corners to create the folds of the bag.

Rounding out the cut edges to give a natural look.

Rounding out the bottom edge of the cake to make it look like it has a curved base. This gives the bag a more realistic feel.

Applying the crumb coat.

Using the flexi smoother to provide a smooth base for the sugar paste to stick to.

Covering the Cake

1. To create the front pocket of the backpack, roll out some sugar paste to approximately 10mm thick and cut a rectangle 15cm × 10cm. Trim and smooth the corners with your fingers to round them off.

2. Apply the rectangle to the front of the cake, being careful not to distort the shape. Use a small amount of water if you have trouble getting it to stick.

3. Next roll out a piece of sugar paste large enough to cover the front of the cake. This should be around 3mm in thickness. Drape the paste over the rolling pin and place it on the cake. Quickly but gently arrange the sugar paste so it covers the sides and the top.

4. Using a smoother, smooth down the sugar paste to remove any finger marks or ridges and to ensure there are no trapped air bubbles. If you discover an air bubble, pierce the sugar paste with an acupuncture pin and gently push out the air. Smooth around the pocket area with the flat edge of the smoother.

5. With your thumb pad, smooth and enhance the bag folds made at the top corners.

6. Cover the back of the cake with another piece of sugar paste and smooth in the same way. Trim the excess paste from the top, sides and base and blend out the side seams using the flexi smoother.

Sugar paste rolled to 10mm in thickness, cut out and with corners rounded for the pocket.

The pocket in position on the cake. Take care not to distort the shape when transferring it to the cake.

Covering the front half of the cake with sugar paste.

Smoothing the sugar paste to remove bumps and air bubbles.

Defining the folds in the bag. You could add extra creases here by gently indenting the paste with the side of you little finger.

Blending the seams using a flexi smoother. Try not to use too much pressure, as this can cause ridges.

Eyelets

1. Once the main body of the bag is covered, it's time to start adding the all-important details. First make eyelets around the top of the bag. Only two are needed, as the bag's flap will be covering the rest. Using the base of a piping tip, make an indent on each side of the front of the bag at the top. Remove the sugar paste from inside these circles with a Dresden tool.

2. Thinly roll out a small amount of black paste and cut two circles with the piping tip. Place these inside the holes and gently press them in with a small ball tool, making a little dip. Take care to cover all the exposed cake.

3. To make the silver trim, roll out a small piece of modelling paste to 2mm thick. Cut two circles with the base of the piping tip, then cut a smaller circle inside each one using a small circle cutter to create a ring. Very carefully remove the excess paste and leave the rings to dry for a few minutes so they maintain their shape.

4. Add a few drops of rejuvenator spirit or vodka to a small amount of the silver lustre dust to make a thick liquid. Test the paint on an excess piece of paste to check the consistency. Paint the rings silver and leave them to dry for a few minutes.

5. Place the silver rings on top of the black circles and very gently press in place, being careful not to flatten them. If the silver dust marks the ivory sugar paste, clean it off using the rejuvenator spirit on a cotton bud.

6. Run the stitching tool around the edges of the top of the bag to add extra detail.

Making the indents for the eyelets with a piping tip.

Filling the indents with black sugar paste to give the impression of a hole.

Cutting the trim for the eyelets. Be careful not to distort the rings as you move them.

Painting the rings with lustre dust mixed with rejuvenator spirit. As the spirit evaporates, the paint will turn back into dust so the excess can be reused.

Fitting the silver trim to the eyelet holes.

Adding detail with the stitching tool. Try to use a consistent amount of pressure as you do this so the stitches are the same depth.

The Front Pocket

1. To add interest to the front of the bag, gently press the quilting tool into the sugar paste on the pocket to mark out the pattern.
2. Run the stitching tool along the marked lines to create a quilted effect.
3. Make the zip for the pocket using the silicone zip mould. First dust the zip mould with cornflour to prevent the paste from sticking. Next firmly press modelling paste into the mould and scrape off the excess. Carefully lift the zip out of the mould. As we need a zip longer than the mould, cut off the split end of the zip so it can be joined to another piece. Repeat this three times until you have enough zip to go around three sides of the pocket. Make a zipper using the mould in the same way.

Silicone Moulds

Dust the mould with cornflour or apply a thin layer of white vegetable fat to stop the paste from sticking to the mould. If the mould is very intricate and the paste proving difficult to remove, place it in the freezer for a few minutes to firm up, making the paste easier to release.

4. Brush the sides of the pocket with a small amount of water and attach the zip and the zipper, carefully lining up each section.
5. Paint the metal centre of the zip and the zipper using the silver lustre dust and rejuvenator spirit mixture.

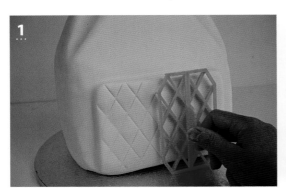
Embossing the pocket with the quilting tool.

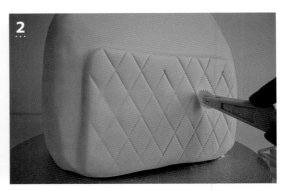
Creating a quilted effect with the stitching tool.

Using the silicone mould to make the zip and zipper with modelling paste.

Attaching the zip to the sides of the pocket.

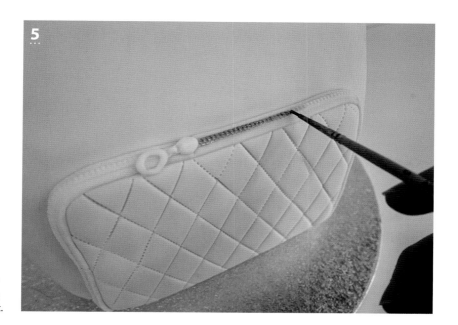

Painting the metal parts of the zip with the lustre dust and rejuvenator spirit paint.

Top Flap and Straps

1. To make the bag flap, roll out the sugar paste to around 3mm thick. Cut out a rectangle slightly narrower than the width of the top of the cake, approximately 10cm wide by 18cm long. Round off the corners and run the stitching tool around the edges.

2. Brush a small amount of water on the back of the top edge of the bag and attach the flap. Let it sit naturally over the creases.

3. Make the fastening button by rolling a small piece of modelling paste in your fingers into a barrel shape. Check the size against the cake and flatten the back slightly to make it easier to attach, then leave it to dry for a few minutes. Attach the button to the cake with a little water. You may need to hold it in place for a few seconds. Paint the fastening with the silver lustre paint mixture.

4. The bag straps need to be a little longer than the bag height. Roll out the sugar paste to 4–5mm thick. Cut two strips of 25cm long by 4–5cm wide. Check the size on the back of the

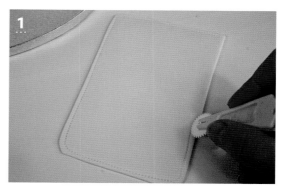

Adding stitching detail to the flap.

Attaching the flap to the top of the bag, letting it sit naturally over the folds for a realistic look.

cake – a little too long is perfect, as they can be trimmed to fit. The straps will attach at the top and drape over the board at the bottom. When you are happy with the size, add stitching detail around the edges.

5. Attach the straps to the top of the bag at the back.

6. Trim the straps so they fit neatly against the base of the cake.

7. Make a small bag handle by cutting a thin strip of paste. Add the stitching detail and attach the handle on top of the straps.

The fastener button is attached to the flap with a small amount of water. If you have trouble getting it to stick, use a small cocktail stick to hold it in place.

Cutting and detailing the bag straps. Make them longer than you need, as they will be trimmed to fit.

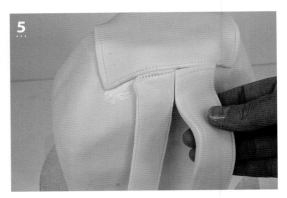

Attaching the straps to the back centre of the backpack with a little water.

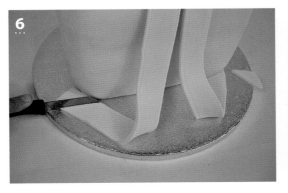

Trimming the strap to fit neatly against the base of the bag.

Making the handle. This could be positioned to cover any imperfections where the straps attach.

Covering the Board

1. To make the draped fabric effect on the board, start by rolling out white sugar paste to around 2mm thick. Drape the paste over the board loosely, creating folds. Work on the front of the board first, then the back, folding the paste over where the two sides meet. You will need to carefully lift the straps as you add the sugar paste.

2. Trim off the excess with a sharp knife, using the edge of the board as a guide.

3. Add a ribbon around the edge of the board, using double-sided tape or a non-toxic glue.

Covering the board using a draping fabric technique. Use the folds to hide any joins.

Trimming the excess, using the edge of the board as a guide.

The completed backpack.

CHAPTER 7

PROJECT 2: USING TEMPLATES

. . . .

For our next project, I have chosen a boot with a flower print. The shape is very easily adapted to different themes such as work boots, wellies or walking boots, and the techniques used for this cake can be applied to almost any type of shoe cake.

This project introduces the use of templates and ganache. Templates are essential for most carved cakes to ensure correct proportions and detail placements. For this cake, I have drawn a template based on boots I own, but I often create templates from pictures found on the internet or photographs. Pictures of the subject from the top, sides and front create the best templates and can be enlarged and printed to the size you require. Scan the template onto your phone or computer and enlarge it to the correct size. Then print it, cut it out and attach it to the cake using cocktail sticks to hold it in place.

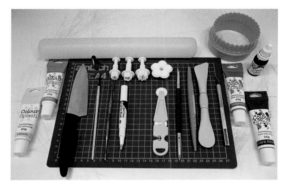

The tools needed for the project.

This project uses ganache to coat the cake instead of buttercream. Ganache sets firm, making the carved cake shape very stable, and it can be levelled out to create a smooth base for the sugar paste. I prefer to use a white chocolate ganache with a vanilla cake, but you could also use milk or dark chocolate.

◀ Project 2: Boot.

Tools and Equipment

Equipment

- 30cm square cake drum
- Offset pallet knife
- Smoother
- Flexi smoother
- Stitching tool
- Craft knife/scalpel
- Serrated knife
- Cerart smoothing tool (optional)
- Rolling pin
- Ruler
- Variety of small flower cutters
- Circle cutter
- Fine paintbrush
- Small piping tip (Wilton #12)
- Dresden tool or silicone-tipped tool
- 15mm ribbon
- Double-sided tape or non-toxic glue

Materials

- Cake (*see* recipes):
      28cm × 13cm, 3 layers
      18cm × 13cm, 1 layer
      15cm × 13cm, 3 layers
- Buttercream, 1 batch
- White chocolate ganache, 1 batch
- 850g black sugar paste
- 650g white sugar paste
- Gel colours: brown, pink, blue, yellow
- Liquid colour: black
- Edible glue/glue pen
- Cornflour for dusting
- 4 tbsp royal icing (made as per package instructions)

METHOD

Carving the Boot

1. Begin by filling and stacking the layers of cake, with the three long layers at the bottom, then the medium layer, then the three shortest layers on top. The ankle section is quite tall and thin, but once covered with ganache, it will become stable. You could place your cake in the freezer for around half an hour at this stage to make it firmer before carving.

2. Attach the template to the side of the cake using cocktail sticks to hold it in place and begin carving the shape. Take off a small amount at a time, just concentrating on the side profile. Remove the template, flip it over and attach it to the other side of the cake and continue to carve. The shape will be refined at a later stage, so do not be too concerned about the details for now.

3. One you are happy with the side profile, start on the top. Take the template for the sole of the boot and place it on the top of the cake. Using the template as a guide for the width of the boot, carve out the shape, keeping the cake a little wider than the template – leave 2cm on each side of the template to allow for adjustment later.

4. You may find it helpful to have a photo or a real boot in front of you for reference while you refine the shape.

5. Start by trimming the corners and straight edges to round them off.

6. Work on the toe area. Keep in mind the cake will be covered with ganache and sugar paste, which will add width, so try not to make it too bulky.

7. The ankle section of the boot tapers to a V shape towards the back but is more rounded down towards the heel.

8. With the knife at a 45-degree angle, trim the bottom edge of the cake. Remember to check your cake from all angles as you carve.

Cake stacked, filled with buttercream and chilled, ready to carve.

Template attached to the cake with cocktail sticks. Begin carving the shape, taking a little off at a time.

With the template as a guide, carve the width of the boot slightly larger than the sole.

Basic shape of the boot carved, ready to be refined.

Rounding the corners on the ankle section.

Trimming the edges of the toe area.

Taper the back of the ankle section for a realistic shape.

Trimming the bottom edge of the cake to give it a rounded appearance.

Covering the cake with white chocolate ganache.

Using the flexi smoother to create a smooth surface for the sugar paste to stick to.

Applying the Ganache

1. Warm the ganache (if necessary) so it has the consistency of peanut butter. Using a small offset pallet knife, quickly apply the ganache to the whole of the cake in an even layer. If you have trouble getting the ganache to stick to your cake (if the cake is crumbling in places), simply dip your pallet knife in hot water for a few seconds before smoothing the ganache on.

2. Once the cake is covered, smooth the ganache with a flexi smoother. Fill any holes or dimples to create a smooth base for the sugar paste to stick to. Again, dip the smoother in hot water if the ganache starts to set too quickly.

3. Chill the cake to set the ganache quickly, or simply leave at room temperature until it is firm. The ganache seals the cake, keeping it fresh, and provides a smooth base for the sugar paste. It also adds flavour and stability.

Covering the Cake

1. Roll out some black sugar paste, large enough to cover the toe area of the boot. Lightly brush the ganache with water and cover the front half of the cake with the sugar paste. Smooth the paste on, using the side of your hand to push it around the bottom of the cake, and trim off the excess.

2. Cut a smaller rectangle of sugar paste to cover the top of the ankle section. Apply, smooth, and again cut off the excess.

3. To make the tongue of the boot, take a piece of black sugar paste 8cm × 14cm in size. Round off the top with the edge of a circle cutter, then place it against the toe section so the top of the tongue is a few centimetres taller than the cake. Smooth the join.

4. The side sections of the boot overlap the tongue so, before they are put in place, the flowers need to be added. Roll four balls of white sugar paste, each roughly the size of a satsuma, and colour one pink, one blue and one yellow, leaving the remaining ball white.

5. Dust the work surface with cornflour and roll out the white sugar paste ball as thinly as possible. Cut out flowers of varying sizes using the flower cutters. Repeat for each colour. Apply the flowers to the cake using a small dab of edible glue, gently pressing the flowers down to make them as flat as possible and give the impression they are part of the fabric.

6. Run the stitching tool around the sides and top of the boot tongue, going across the flowers where they are near the edge.

7. Roll out a large rectangle of black sugar paste around 20cm × 30cm. Working on one side of the cake, brush the ganache lightly with water and apply the sugar paste. Trim the paste down the centre of the back of the cake, and halfway between the toe and the tongue section, leaving the overhang at the top of the cake.

Trim the excess paste on the tongue, leaving enough space to add the eyelets (2–3cm). Do not stick this down, as it needs to be lifted slightly to add the eyelets and laces. Remove the excess paste from the bottom edge.

8. While carefully holding the sugar paste at the top of the ankle section, trim it, leaving an overhang slightly taller than the tongue.

9. Repeat on the other side of the boot and add the remaining flowers.

Covering the front half of the cake with black sugar paste.

Covering and removing the excess sugar paste on the top of the ankle section.

Black sugar paste rolled out and cut to create the boot tongue. The top is cut with the edge of the circle cutter.

Smoothing the join.

Flowers cut out ready to be attached to the cake.

Attaching the flowers using edible glue.

Using the stitching tool on the tongue.

Covering the side with black sugar paste.

Cutting the paste at the back of the boot.

Trimming the side of the boot.

Cutting out the semicircle shape on the side.

Cutting the excess sugar paste at the top, so it's slightly taller than the tongue.

Trimming the other side of the boot.

Adding the remaining flowers.

Adding the Details

1. The secret to taking your work to the next level is the detail. Add a double line of stitching around side of the boot and a single line up the middle, on both sides. Then add stitching around the inside and the outside of the ankle section.

2. Add some creases to the back of the boot using a tool or the side of your hand, and on the toe of the boot where it would naturally bend when walking.

3. To make the seam at the back of the boot, roll out some black sugar paste and cut a strip 23cm long and 2cm wide. Add stitching around the edges on both sides. Attach the strip to the back centre of the boot using some edible glue so that it sits over the join. Loop over the top

Applying stitching to the eyelets section.

Adding stitching detail to the inside.

Using the stitching tool on the ankle section.

Adding creases to the back and side of the boot.

Creating creases where the toe section would naturally bend.

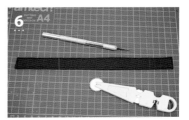

Black sugar paste rolled and cut into a strip to make the back seam.

The strip glued to the back of the boot.

Loop created by folding over the top of the strip and gluing it down level with the stitching detail.

Making holes for the eyelets with the piping tip.

Scoring the black sugar paste strip to create the sole trim.

Apply the trim round the bottom of the boot with edible glue.

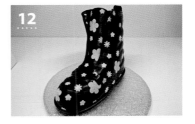

Steaming the cake gives a clean and glossy appearance.

of the strip and stick it down in line with the stitching on the ankle.

4. Create the eyelets for the laces by cutting holes with a Wilton #12 piping tip. Support the sugar paste with your finger and gently push the tip through. Continue up the boot, making sure that the eyelets on each side are opposite each other. You may find it easier cutting them out in pairs.

5. Roll out a long strip of sugar paste to 5mm thick and 2cm wide. Using a pointed tool, score lines

across the strip to create the edge of the rubber sole. Starting at the toe of the boot, wrap the strip around the cake. Cut a small triangle for the heel of the boot. Steam the boot to give a satin appearance.

Covering the Board

1. Before adding the laces and final details, we need to cover the board and move the boot to its final position. I have chosen to create a wooden floor effect for this project as it can be used for many different themed cakes. To begin, take the remaining white sugar paste and add some brown gel colour. Knead the paste until it has just started to colour, creating a marbled effect.

2. Roll out the paste wide enough to cover the board and brush the board lightly with some water. Place the sugar paste on the board and smooth it down.

3. Create floorboards by scoring lines across the board equal distances apart, in a brickwork pattern. Draw finer lines to create the wood grain effect and paint with a few drops of gel colour mixed with a little water. The paint

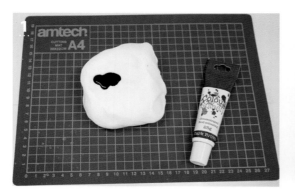

Brown gel colour applied to white sugar paste.

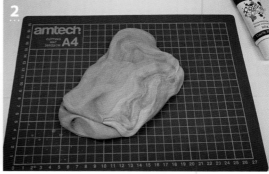

The sugar paste is kneaded until the brown colour starts to show, creating a marbled effect.

The marbled brown sugar paste rolled out to cover the cake drum.

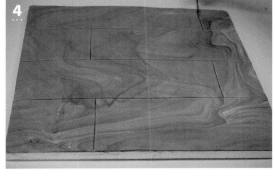

Lines added to create floorboards.

Finer lines scored in to create a woodgrain effect.

Painting the board with a gel colour and water mixture.

will fill the indents of the lines, enhancing the wood grain.

4. Carefully lift the cake from your workboard and into position. The board will be quite sticky from the water and gel mixture so take care when placing the cake down. Leave the board to dry fully before continuing.

Final Touches

1. Roll some black sugar paste into a long thin sausage shape, or use an extruder if you have one available. The laces should be around 2–3mm thick so they can be threaded through the eyelets.

2. Start with the bottom part of the laces, securing them with the edible glue. Use a silicone-tipped tool to push the ends of the laces into the eyelets. Thread the laces through the holes in a criss-cross pattern for a realistic look. Secure the laces with a dab of glue in the centre if needed. Leave the ends of the laces long and hanging down.

3. Using a fine brush, paint along all the stitching with black liquid food colour to create the thread.

4. Colour a small amount of royal icing with the yellow gel colour and place it in a piping bag. Snip the end to make a small opening and pipe yellow stitching around the sole. Try to keep the stiches and spacing equal.

5. Finally, add a ribbon to the edge of the cake board with non-toxic glue or double-sided tape.

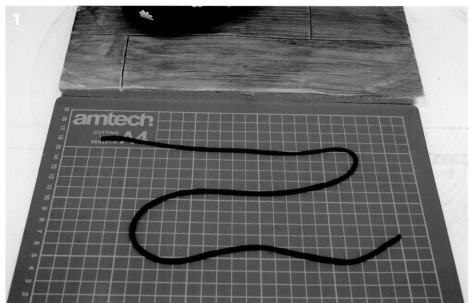

Black sugar paste rolled to make the laces.

Using the silicone-tipped tool to push the lace into the eyelet.

Attaching the lace in a criss-cross pattern, threading it through the eyelets where possible.

The ends of the laces are left to hang down. Secure with a small dab of glue if necessary.

Stitching detail is enhanced with black liquid colour.

Piping the yellow stitching on the top edge of the sole.

The completed cake.

CHAPTER 8

PROJECT 3: CARVING VEHICLES

· ·

Car cakes are an extremely popular choice for birthdays and are not as difficult as they may seem. The most important aspect is the shape, and you can ensure you get that right by using a template. Pay close attention to the details on the car and add a personalised number plate for that bespoke touch.

This cake needs no supporting structure. The illusion that the cake is sitting on wheels is created with the carving. If you go on to make other vehicles with greater ground clearance, such as a tractor or monster truck, you will need to add a platform to raise the cake off the board; this is covered later in the book.

The techniques in this project can be adapted to create any vehicle, from tanks or trucks to trains.

The tools needed for the project.

◀ Project 3: Car.

Tools and Equipment

Tools
- 30cm square cake drum
- Offset pallet knife
- Smoother
- Flexi smoother
- Craft knife/scalpel
- Serrated knife
- Rolling pin
- Ruler
- Small circle cutter
- Piping tip equivalent in size to the wheels
- Piping tip slightly smaller than the wheels
- Fine paintbrush
- Dresden tool or silicone-tipped tool
- Knife tool
- Ball tool
- Steamer
- Cocktail sticks
- Aluminium foil
- 15mm ribbon
- Double-sided tape or non-toxic glue

Materials
- Cake (*see* Chapter 5):
    - 33cm × 18cm, 2 layers
    - 20cm × 18cm, 1 layer
- Buttercream, 1 batch
- 150g black sugar paste
- 450g white sugar paste
- Gel colour: red, orange, yellow
- Dust colours: black and silver
- Dipping solution/alcohol
- Edible glue/glue pen
- Cornflour for dusting

METHOD

Carving the Cake

1. Print and cut out the provided templates (enlarging them to the correct size).
2. Begin the cake by filling and stacking the first two (larger) layers of the sponge. Use the side-view template (template 1) to determine the position of the final layer, which will make the car's roof.
3. Attach template 1 to the cake using the cocktail sticks and begin carving the car shape using a large serrated knife. Be careful to keep the knife flat as you carve, so the car is an even height on both sides.
4. Holding a small knife at a 45-degree angle, cut away the base of the cake between the wheels on both sides, and on the front and back of the car.
5. Attach the top-view template (template 2) to the top and cut the width.
6. As shown on the front- and end-view templates (templates 3 and 4), the sides of the car slope in towards the centre. To create this angle, first mark the top edge of the window with cocktail sticks. Then attach template 3 to the front of the cake, making sure it lines up with template 2. Carefully lift template 2 from the top of the cake, leaving the cocktail stick markers in place.
7. Score the side of the cake at the car's widest point using template 3 as a guide. Angle the knife from the cocktail sticks and trim down to the score line. Use the template as a

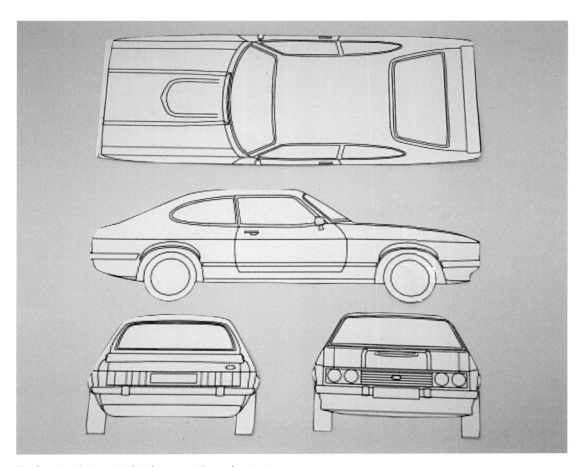

The four templates printed to the correct size and cut out.

guide to cut the lower section. Repeat on the other side.

8. The car we are creating has a dipped section in the centre of the bonnet, marked in green on template 2 in the photo. As in step 6, mark the width of the dip with the cocktail sticks then remove the template.

9. Using a small serrated knife, score the edges of the section and gently carve with the flat side of the blade. Do not carve too deeply – a few millimetres is sufficient. Check the shape from all angles and make any adjustments if needed.

Stacked vanilla sponge cakes filled with buttercream, ready to begin carving.

Attach template 1 to the side of the cake with cocktail sticks to use as a guide for carving the car shape. Keep the knife flat as you carve so the car height is even on both sides.

Carving the base edge of the car to create the illusion that the car is raised off the board.

The carved cake after carving around template 1.

Attach template 2 to the top of the cake to carve the width of the car.

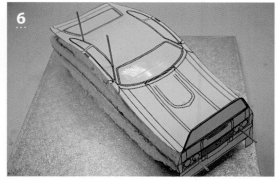

Attach template 3 to the front of the cake and insert cocktails sticks in the top as markers to show where the slant of the side begins.

Lift off template 2 carefully, leaving the markers in place.

Score the side of the cake at its widest part as a guide for cutting the angle.

Carving the cake at an angle to create the side shape of the car.

Cutting the angle for the bottom section of the car.

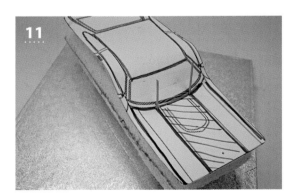

Cocktail sticks mark the width of the dip in the bonnet.

Use the side of the knife to carve out the dip, being careful not to carve too deeply.

The carved bonnet with the edges rounded slightly.

Check the cake from all angles.

Applying the Crumb Coat

I used buttercream for this project as the cake does not need any extra stability. For a taller vehicle, ganache would be more suitable.

1. Cover the cake with a layer of buttercream, using an offset pallet knife.
2. A smooth base is particularly important on this cake and can be achieved using a flexi smoother.

Applying a crumb coat of buttercream to trap the crumbs and create a smooth base.

Smoothing the buttercream with a flexi smoother to create a smooth base for the sugar paste to stick to.

Cutting out the Wheels

Using template 1 as a guide, cut out the circles for the wheels, 1cm deep, with the base of a large piping tip. Apply butter cream to the cavities and chill the cake until the butter-cream is firm.

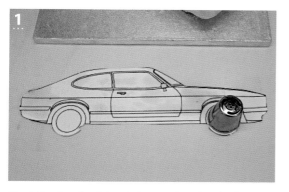

Check the size of a piping tip base against the wheels on the template.

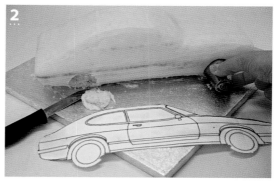

Cutting the circles for the wheels using the large piping tip base, to a depth of 5mm.

Applying the crumb coat to the wheel cavities.

Covering the Cake

1. Weigh out 300g of the white sugar paste and colour it with the red colour gel. If the paste becomes sticky, wrap it in clingfilm and leave it to rest for 5 minutes or so.

2. Roll out the sugar paste to approximately 2mm thick and cover the cake. Smooth out the paste, pushing it under the bottom edge of the car.

3. Trim off the excess.

Sugar paste coloured with the red gel colour. Wrap the paste and leave it to rest if it becomes sticky.

Covering the car with the red sugar paste.

Trimming off the excess sugar paste after smoothing it under the car.

Bodywork Details

1. Gently hold template 1 on the side of the car, making sure the wheels line up and the template is straight. Using the Dresden tool, draw over all the lines (including the windows), lightly embossing the sugar paste. Remove the template and go over the markings with a small knife tool.

2. Repeat step 1 using the top, front and back templates on the car.

3. On the front of the car, cut out the grille and remove the red sugar paste.

4. Roll out a small piece of black sugar paste and cut out the rectangle for the grille, using the template as a guide. Stick the black rectangle in place with a small amount of edible glue and smooth it down with a small spatula tool.

5. Make indents for the headlights using the small end of the ball tool. Roll out a small piece of white sugar paste and cut four circles with the small circle cutter. Stick the circles over the indents and press each one with the ball tool, making a small dip.

6. Etch the grille lines with the knife tool.

7. Cut a long strip of black sugar paste, using template 1 as a guide for the width. Apply the strip, starting between the wheels. Cut the excess and add the line details. Continue placing the strip all the way around the car, adding the detail as you go.

Embossing the lines of the car with a tool. Gently hold the template in place to avoid marking the car.

Enhance the embossed lines using the knife tool.

Adding the lines to the bonnet. Do not press too deeply.

8. Add a few drops of dipping solution or alcohol to a little black dust to create a liquid paint. Paint the windows with a fine paintbrush, using your little finger to stabilise your hand as you work. Lightly steam the cake to seal the dust colour. Roll a very thin tube of black sugar paste to edge the windows. Attach it with a tiny amount of edible glue if it is needed, taking care not to smudge the black dust colour.

Removing the red sugar paste from the front of the car.

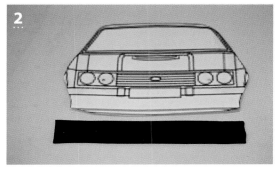

Black sugar paste cut to the shape of the grille using template 3 as a guide.

Placing the black sugar paste rectangle in the cut-out area for the grille and smoothing it with a small spatula tool. The red sugar paste should slightly overhang the black.

Making four indents for the headlights using the small ball tool.

Adding the headlights and indenting each one with the ball tool to make it concave.

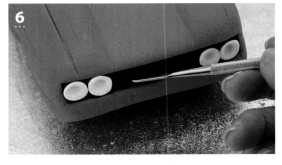

Creating the grille with the knife tool.

9. Take 10g of white sugar paste and colour it with the orange gel colour. Cut two small rectangles of the resulting orange sugar paste for the indicators and attach them to the front bumper, below the headlights.

10. Roll out some white sugar paste and cut a rectangle for the number plate. Using the black dust and dipping solution method, add the numbers and letters of your choice. Leave the number plate to dry for a few minutes before

Attaching the black strip of sugar paste to the car for the side trim and removing the excess.

Adding the lines to the black side trim strip.

Continue the black strip all the way around the car, checking that it is straight and even.

Painting the windows with dust mixed with dipping solution.

Adding the window trim with finely rolled black sugar paste.

Add orange rectangles for the indicators.

A rectangle of white sugar paste painted with black dust paint makes the bespoke number plate, attached with glue, between the indicators.

Add a yellow number plate to the back of the car.

Applying edible glue around the base of the cake.

Smoothing on the strip of black paste around the bottom of the cake to create depth. Line the strip to the bottom edge of the car.

Using a silicone tool to push the black strip to the bottom of the car.

Trimming away the excess sugar paste from the bottom of the cake.

attaching it to the centre of the font bumper with some edible glue. Colour 5g of white sugar paste with the yellow colour gel and repeat these steps to make a yellow number plate and orange lights for the back of the car.

11. To give the impression that the car is sitting on wheels instead of the board, we need to add the illusion of depth under the car. Roll out the black sugar paste to 1mm in thickness and cut a long strip 3cm wide. Apply edible glue to the bottom edge of the car on all sides and add the black strip, lining it up to where the bottom of the car would be. Push the sugar paste against the bottom of the cake and cut off the excess.

Texturing the Board

1. Before the wheels can be added, the board needs to be covered. Take the remaining white sugar paste and 20g of black gel and mix them together. Create a slight marbled effect by kneading the paste until it turns grey, leaving visible colour streaks.

2. Roll out the grey sugar paste to 2mm thick and place it on the board, pressing the paste under the car. Cut the excess and cover the back half of the board, smoothing the seams. Press a piece of crumpled aluminium foil into the surface of the board to create a concrete texture. Edge the board with some ribbon, using non-toxic glue or double-sided tape.

Covering the board with the marbled grey sugar paste. Push the paste up to the car edge. No need to worry about fingerprints, as the texture will hide any imperfections.

Creating texture on the board with crumpled up foil. Try varying the pressure of the foil for extra interest.

Adding the Wheels

1. Roll out the remaining black sugar paste to 5mm thick. Cut four circles using the large piping-tip base previously used for cutting out the wheel shapes from the cake. Indent the edge of each wheel with the knife tool to make the tyre tracks. With the smaller piping-tip base, mark a circle on each of the wheels to make the hubcaps. Paint the hubcaps with silver dust and dipping solution.

2. While the hubcaps dry, use the silver dust paint to add some interest to the windows. Three quick diagonal lines in the left-hand corner of each window give the illusion of light. It is these details that will take the cake to the next level!

Cutting out the wheels with the large piping tip base.

Creating tyre tracks with the knife tool.

Marking the hubcaps with a smaller piping tip base. Use a ball tool or the end of a paintbrush to make a dimple in the centre.

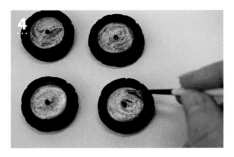

Painting the hubcaps with silver dust paint. The wheels will need to dry for a few minutes before being attached.

Creating light reflections on the windows with the silver dust paint.

Final Touches

Apply edible glue to the back of each of the wheels and add them to the car. Take a pea-sized piece of black sugar paste and roll it into a rectangle for the car door handles. Make one for each side and place them on the cake using the side-view template as a guide for the correct position. To make the wing mirrors, shape a small piece of red sugar paste into a rectangle and attach it to the corner of the door using the edible glue. Repeat for the other side.

Finally, steam the cake to give a glossy appearance.

Adding the final details of the door handles and wing mirrors, then giving the cake a steam to create a glossy appearance. You could also spray the car with a confectioner's glaze spray for extra shine.

The completed car cake.

CHAPTER 9

PROJECT 4: SIMPLE STRUCTURE

. . . .

The next project is a sitting dog cake. Animal cakes are as popular as ever among adults and children and can be made for any occasion. The techniques needed for this project can be used to make any breed of dog, cat or other sitting four-legged animal.

This project uses simple dowel supports for the structure. I use plastic easy-cut dowels (poly-dowels), but wooden ones would also be suitable.

Templates are provided for the dog's front and side views and for the boards needed for support.

The tools needed for the project.

◀ The completed cake.

Tools and Equipment

Tools

- 30cm square cake drum
- 3mm cake card
- Small hacksaw/scissors
- Aluminium foil tape
- Offset pallet knife
- Smoothing tool
- Flexi smoother
- Craft knife/scalpel
- Serrated knives, large and small
- Ruler
- Rolling pin
- Fine paintbrush
- 25mm paintbrush
- Dresden tool or silicone-tipped tool
- Ball tool
- Writing piping tip or small circle cutter
- Stitching tool
- Small ramekin
- Raking tool
- Poly-dowels
- Steamer
- Cocktail sticks
- Small blender
- 15mm ribbon
- Double-sided tape or non-toxic glue

Materials

- Cake (*see* Chapter 5):
    - 18cm-diameter round, 5 layers
    - 15cm-diameter round, 3 layers
    - 13cm × 10cm, 2 layers
    - 9cm × 10cm, 1 layer
- Buttercream, 2 batches
- Ganache, 1 batch
- 20g black sugar paste
- 1.5kg white sugar paste
- Gel colour: red, brown, koala, white
- Dust colours: black, green
- Dipping solution/alcohol
- Edible glue/glue pen
- Cornflour for dusting

You may wish to find a reference photo online for the facial features.

METHOD

The Support Structure

1. Begin by tracing the templates for the boards onto 3mm cake card and carefully cut them out with a small hacksaw. Cover the cut edges with aluminium foil tape to stop any card pieces getting onto the cake and to make the board food safe. Stack and fill the 18cm-diameter cakes using the template to determine the position, staggering each one slightly. Be careful not to make this section lean too much. It should be stable and stand without support.

2. To add the first support board, use the template to see where the board will sit and lightly score around it to mark it on the cake. Remove the board and add four dowels in a cross formation. Push each dowel straight down to the cake drum and make a small mark with an edible pen where the excess needs cutting. Remove the dowel from the cake and score the cut line. Snap the dowel to get a clean break. If you are using wooden dowels, cut with a hacksaw.

3. Cover the top cake layer in ganache. Place the board over the dowels, pressing down to check the support level.

4. Spread ganache on the top of the board and add the first 15cm-diameter layer. Continue stacking and filling the 15cm layers with the buttercream. Use the template to determine the position of the head support board and temporarily stick it down with a little buttercream.

The cakes filled and stacked ready to carve with the support cake board in position.

Insert dowels to provide support for the board.

Attach the cake board with a thin layer of buttercream.

The remaining layers of cake are filled and stacked. Hold the neck support board lightly in position with a small dab of buttercream.

Making the structure food safe

Any surface that comes into contact with the cake must be made food safe. This means that the materials used will not contaminate the food and do not pose any health risks.

To make an element such as a threaded rod food safe, a barrier between the rod and the cake must be applied. This can be plastic wrap, cling film, foil, or a plastic drinking straw. An edible barrier such as melted chocolate can also be used, but it must not be eaten.

Carving the Body

1. Using the template, carve the back of the dog with the large serrated knife. Start from the head board, as this is the neck of the dog. The back should have a gentle curve down to the base. Next, reduce bulk on the sides by carving down from the head board to about halfway down the body, taking small amounts off.

2. Attach the front template to the front of the cake with cocktail sticks. Notice where the back legs of the dog are wider than the rest of the body. Carve down to the wider leg section and remove the template. Using the small serrated knife, shape the back legs so they are rounded and flow naturally from the body.

3. Shape around the bottom of the cake so it curves under, creating a more realistic appearance. Keep refining the shape, checking it from all angles. Save the offcuts as they will be needed further on in the project.

4. Insert four dowels for the head board, taking care they do not pop out of the front of the cake.

Begin carving the cake using the template as a guide, starting with the slope of the back.

Carve down from the neck board.

Using the template, carve the width of the dog. Note the position of the back legs.

Carving and rounding off the back legs.

Round off the base of the cake, trimming the cake at a 45-degree angle.

Refine the shape, checking the cake from all angles.

Add dowels to the neck area to support the cake board. Take care not to place them too far forward or they may pop out of the front of the chest area.

Carving the Head

1. Fill and stack the remaining cake layers and attach the head support board to the bottom of the cake with ganache. Carve out from the board at a 45-degree angle to allow the board shape to be seen once it is right side up.

2. Cut the head and ears from the two templates and use them to carve the head shape. Make two indents where the eyes will go.

Cake filled and stacked ready to carve the head.

Attach the neck board with ganache and turn the cake over. Carve out from the board so the shape is visible.

Using the front and side templates, carve the shape of the dog's head.

Make two indents for the eyes using a ball tool.

Applying Ganache

1. Using an offset pallet knife, apply a layer of ganache over the body and the head. Smooth the ganache with the flexi smoother, creating a smooth base for the sugar paste to stick to, and adding stability. Allow the ganache to fully set, either in the fridge or at room temperature, before continuing.

2. Once the ganache has set, apply a layer on the neck and add the head cake. Add extra ganache to the join and smooth with the flexi smoother. Leave to set firm.

Cover the cake with a layer of ganache.

Use a flexi smoother to create a smooth base for the sugar paste to stick to.

Cover the head with ganache and attach it to the body. Apply more ganache around the neck and smooth it down to keep the head securely attached.

The Head

If you do not require many servings or the subject has a large, heavy head, it could be made from polystyrene or Rice Krispie treats (RKT). These alternatives are a lot lighter than cake and allow for awkward shapes to be created. Both RKT and polystyrene can be carved and covered in the same way as cake.

Cake Clay

To create the back paws, make up a batch of cake clay. Cake clay is a mixture of cake and buttercream, which – as the name suggests – can be sculpted like clay. It can also be used to correct any carving mistakes. If too much cake is taken away, then cake clay can be added onto the cake so carving can continue. Leftovers can be made into cake pops.

Back Paws

1. Take a large handful of cake offcuts and few dollops of buttercream and mix them together. This is a messy job, so wear gloves! The resulting 'clay' should stay together when squashed into a ball shape. If it does not, add more buttercream. It can also be made with ganache.
2. Take a ball of the clay and shape it into the back paw using the template as a guide for the size. Repeat for the other foot and cover both paws with ganache.

Cake clay is a mixture of cake offcuts and buttercream, and should hold its shape when squeezed together.

Cake clay used to sculpt the back paws.

Covering the Cake and Creating Fur Texture

1. Roll out the white sugar paste to a thickness of 3mm in a sheet large enough to cover the body of the dog. Brush the body section with some water and apply the sugar paste. Trim the excess sugar paste and smooth the seams.
2. Using a Dresden or silicone-tipped tool, lightly draw a line down the centre of the dog's back to indicate the spine. The fur falls either side of the spine, down towards the paws. With the tool, draw S shapes, varying the depth and size to create a fur texture over the entire body.
3. To make fluffy feet, pull the sugar paste down onto the cake drum with the silicone-tipped tool. This technique can also be used at the base of the body and later for the tail.

Applying white sugar paste to the body of the dog. Brush the ganache with a small amount of water if it will not stick.

Blend the seams with a smoothing tool.

Create the fur texture with the Dresden tool. Draw S-shaped lines at varying depths and lengths.

Fuzzy feet are created by pulling the sugar paste down onto the board with a silicone-tipped tool.

Front Legs, Paws and Tail (Illustrations overleaf)

1. Take two dowels and measure them against the cake, to ensure they will not pierce through the back. Cut them to size and insert them at an angle into the cake where the front legs sit. These dowels will also add stability to the cake.
2. Roll a column of sugar paste the same length as the dowel. Make a cut halfway down the length of the sugar paste column and brush some edible glue on each side of the incision. Gently pull apart the sugar paste to allow it to wrap around the dowel and smooth the seam at the back and top. Shape the paw and add the fur texture. Repeat for the other leg.
3. Roll a thick column of sugar paste for the tail. Draw a line down the centre of the tail and pull out the sugar paste with the silicone-tipped tool, as in previous steps. Attach the tail with edible glue.

Insert dowels in the chest area for the front legs and to help support the body.

Roll out sugar paste into a cylinder to make the front legs, and make a cut lengthways down the middle so it can be fitted around the dowel.

Attach the leg around the dowel with a little edible glue and sculpt the paw.

Create fur texture on the leg and paw using the silicone-tipped tool.

Add fur texture to the tail using the same technique as on the feet.

Attach the tail to the body using edible glue and blend with the fur texture.

The Head and Facial Features

1. Roll a sausage shape 2cm in diameter and flatten with your fingers. With some edible glue, attach the strip in the middle at the nose area in a W shape to create the muzzle.

2. Cover the head with white sugar paste, smoothing around the muzzle to make a mouth area. Using your thumbs, gently make soft indents either side down from the eyes to the side of the muzzle. Add a light fur texture with the raking tool.

3. With the ball tool, deepen the eye sockets. Make a small amount of brown sugar paste with the brown gel colour and roll it into two balls. Place the eyes in the sockets, slicing off the backs to flatten them if they are too prominent. Mark the pupils with a writing tip or small circle cutter and paint with black dust and dipping solution. Add a small dot of white in the pupil as light reflections. This brings life to the eyes.

4. Add a small sliver of white sugar paste to the lower eye to create the eyelid. Smooth it on with the silicone-tipped tool and feather it out to make the fur texture. Repeat on the upper lid. Roll a teardrop shape for the eyebrow and flatten slightly. Apply it above the eye and add texture. Repeat for the other side.

5. For the nose, take a small ball of black sugar paste and shape it into a rounded triangle using your fingers and thumb, and attach it with a dab of edible glue. With the flat end of the Dresden tool, make a C shape for the nostrils. Draw a line down the centre of the nose and continue it down the muzzle. Draw a small line for the mouth. Add some dots for the markings around the nose.

6. Roll out the remaining white sugar paste and cut two triangles, each 11cm tall. Apply glue to the back, bottom edge of the triangle and attach it to the head, folding it forwards. Gently bring

A rolled and flattened strip of sugar paste to create the lip and muzzle area.

Attach the strip of sugar paste with edible glue in a W shape to create the muzzle.

Cover the head in white sugar paste, smoothing around the muzzle.

Use your thumbs to make indents down the side of the nose.

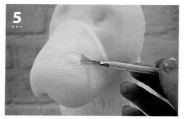

Add a light fur texture to the face using the raking tool.

Two balls of brown sugar paste make the eyes; mark the pupils with a piping tip.

Paint the pupils with back dust and dipping solution. A white dot gives the impression of light reflection.

Add sugar paste to the bottom of the eye for the eyelid and blend it in with the fur texture effect.

Adding the top eyelid.

Add a teardrop-shape piece of sugar paste above the eye to form the eyebrow area and apply fur texture with the silicone-tipped tool.

A black rounded triangle of sugar paste is used for the nose and attached with edible glue.

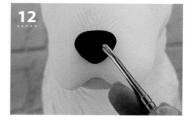

Mark the nostrils with the Dresden tool in a curved C shape.

Adding nose and mouth lines with the Dresden tool.

Making dots around the nose with a pointed tool; you could use the end of a paintbrush instead.

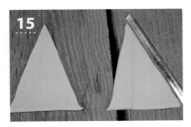

Sugar paste thinly rolled out and cut into triangles for the ears.

Apply edible glue to the base of the ear, then attach it to the head and fold it forward.

Fold the ear gently forward until it is resting on the side of the face.

the ear towards the front so it hangs down the side of the face. Round off the edges of the sugar paste to make the ears look more natural.

Colouring the Dog

1. In a small ramekin, mix a few drops of the koala-colour gel with a little water. Paint the dog with a 25mm paintbrush, a section at a time. Do not get the sugar paste too wet, as the water will begin to remove the texture and the sugar paste will get very sticky. Use a smaller brush on the face, taking care around the eyes and nose. Allow the cake to dry fully before continuing. The cake will be sticky while it is drying, so try not to touch it.

2. Once the cake is completely dry, add some black dust around the nose, dabbing the excess on a paper towel.

3. Paint the waterline of the eyes and the mouth with black dust and dipping solution and add some shading with the brown dust around the edge of the ears.

Painting the dog with gel colour mixed with water, using a large paintbrush.

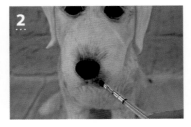

Painting details on the face with black dust.

Painting the mouth with dust and dipping solution.

The Bandana and Covering the Board

1. Colour the remaining sugar paste with the red gel colour. Roll it out to around 2mm and cut an elongated V shape for the bandana.
2. Use the stitching tool along the edges and place the bandana around the neck of the dog. Cross over the ends and leave them to hang on the back of the neck. The bandana would be the perfect place to add a name or message for a birthday or, alternatively, a collar with a tag could be made.

3. A quick yet effective way to cover a board is with cake crumb grass. First edge the board with ribbon using non-toxic glue. This will help keep the crumbs on the board. Take a handful of cake offcuts, preferably without buttercream, and put them in the blender with a pinch of green dust colour. The crumbs will turn green to create grass. Paint the board with edible glue or piping gel and sprinkle on the 'grass', covering all the silver of the board. Any green crumbs on the dog can be dusted off with a paint brush. This technique can also be used to create soil by switching the green dust for brown.

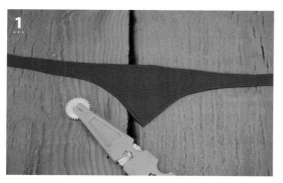

The bandana shape is cut out of rolled out red sugar paste and a stitching effect is created with the stitching tool.

The bandana is put in place and secured with the edible glue.

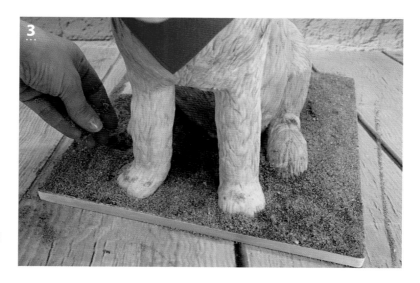

Sprinkle cake offcuts blended with green dust colour over the board to create a grass effect. Add a ribbon to the edge of the board with non-toxic glue.

CHAPTER 10

PROJECT 5: STANDING STRUCTURE

• • • • • • • • • •

The next project introduces the use of a standing structure, in this case to create a cartoon-style astronaut; the structure could be used to make any standing character.

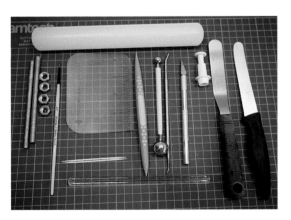

Tools needed for the standing structure project.

For this structure I have used steel threaded rods as opposed to PVC pipe, as the cake is quite narrow at the base. Using the template, determine where the structure will need to stand and measure the rods, leaving space to allow for the boards, washers and nuts. Threaded rod can easily be cut with a jeweller's saw. Use a vice to clamp the rod to the workbench to save your hands, as the threads can be quite sharp!

> ## Tools and Materials
>
> **Tools**
> - 30cm square MDF board
> - 8cm-diameter round MDF board
> - 12cm-diameter round MDF board
> - 18cm M8 threaded rod × 2
>
> (continued overleaf)

◀ Project 5: The finished astronaut cake.

- M8 washers × 12
- M8 nuts × 12
- Aluminium foil tape
- Furniture feet pads/foam board
- Offset pallet knife
- Smoothing tool
- Craft knife/scalpel
- Serrated knives, large and small
- Flexi smoother
- Ruler
- Rolling pin
- Fine paintbrush
- Dresden or silicone-tipped tool
- Ball tool
- Small circle cutter
- Steamer
- Cocktail sticks or bamboo skewers
- Clingfilm
- 15mm ribbon
- Double-sided tape or non-toxic glue

Extra Equipment
- Drill
- Jeweller's saw
- Vice/clamp
- Coping saw (to cut the MDF board)
- Adjustable spanner

Materials
- Cake (*see* Chapter 5):
    - 13cm-diameter round, 3 layers
    - 15cm-diameter round, 2 layers
    - 10cm-diamter round, 1 layer
    - 9cm-diameter round, 2 layers
- Buttercream, 1 batch
- Ganache, 1 batch
- 1.5kg white sugar paste
- 200g black sugar paste
- Dust colour: red, blue, silver, green, white
- Dipping solution/alcohol
- Edible glue/glue pen
- Cornflour for dusting

METHOD

Building the Structure

1. To begin this cake, we must first make the structure. Place the template on the board in the required position and mark the placement of the rods. With an 8mm drill bit, drill the two holes for the rods into the baseboard.

2. Use these holes as a template to drill the holes in the 8cm and 12cm round boards, making sure they are central and that the three boards line up. To make the round boards food safe, cover both sides with aluminium foil tape.

3. Flip the baseboard over and stick on foam furniture feet pads in each of the corners. Polystyrene, foam board or wooden blocks could also be used. These pads will raise the board up, so there is space for the rods to be screwed in place. They are also useful when making a particularly heavy cake, giving space to get your fingers under the board when lifting.

4. Place the threaded rod through one of the holes in the baseboard, and add a washer then a nut to the bottom of the rod. Thread a washer and nut on the top of the rod and finger tighten the nut while holding the one underneath still. Tighten the nuts with an adjustable spanner so the rod is completely secure. Repeat for the other hole.

5. Using the template, measure where the first platform sits and add nuts and washers to the rods. Push the 8cm board onto the rods and add the top washers and nuts. Tighten with the spanner, making sure the board is level.

6. Cover the baseboard with the foil tape so the sugar paste will stick to it. As no cake will touch the rods below the first platform, they do not need to be made food safe.

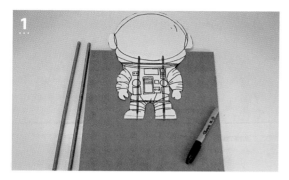

Marking the rod positions before drilling the holes in the baseboard.

Holes drilled in the three boards and the smallest one covered with foil tape.

Furniture pads are attached to the underside of the baseboard to allow space for the rods and nuts.

Tightening the nuts on the underside with an adjustable spanner.

Using the spanner to secure the rods on the top of the baseboard.

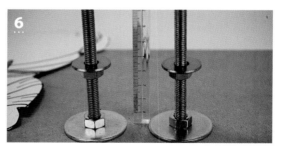

Measuring the placement of the nuts and washers for the lower platform.

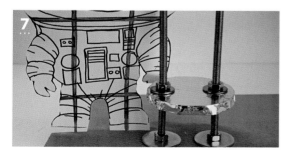

Position the lower platform and secure it with washers and nuts, ensuring it is level.

Covering the Board

1. Take 300g of white sugar paste and knead it together with 20g of black sugar paste to create a grey marbled effect. Shape the sugar paste into a square and gently pull it until it is large enough to cover the board. We are looking for a bumpy, uneven planet surface effect.

2. Make several craters using a large ball tool, and some smaller surrounding ones with the end of a paint brush. Scrunch up some foil and push it into the surface to create a cracked texture. Paint the craters with black dust to give them some depth.

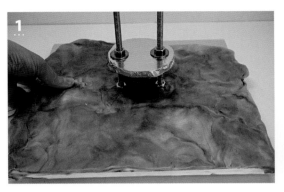

Cover the board by pulling the marbled sugar paste rather than rolling it to achieve an uneven, bumpy look.

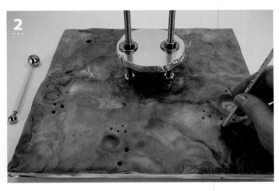

Creating craters using the ball tool and the end of a paintbrush.

Rolled-up foil pushed into the sugar paste creates interesting textures, giving the effect of a dry, cracked ground.

Painting the craters with black dust gives them depth.

Making the Astronaut

1. To make the legs, roll two sausage shapes of white sugar paste to around 3cm in diameter and 6cm long. Shape the foot and make a cut vertically down the back halfway through the centre. Fix each leg around the rods with edible glue and smooth the seams.

2. Add the crease details to the legs using the silicone-tipped tool. Paint the red stripe and the bottom of the boots with silver, mixing the dust with dipping solution.

3. Checking against the template, measure 8cm up from the small round board and add the nuts, washers and the 12cm board. Thread on the washer and nuts and tighten with the spanner, ensuring the board is level. Cover the rods, nut and washers with the foil tape to make them food safe. No metal should come into contact with the cake.

4. Cover the baseboard and legs with clingfilm to protect it while the cake is carved.

5. Add the first of the 9cm round cakes to the lower board with a dab of ganache. Make a cut down the centre of the cake and slide it over the rods. Alternatively, cut the cake in half and stick it back together around the rods with some buttercream.

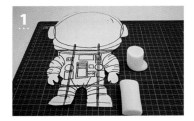

Making the legs by rolling tubes of sugar paste and pinching each one out to form the foot.

Drawing creasing details on the leg with the silicone-tipped tool.

Painting the red and silver details om the legs and boots.

Add the second platform, ensuring it is secure and level.

Covering the board in clingfilm helps to protect it when carving the cake. Make the rods and fittings food safe with foil tape.

Filling and stacking the cakes on the lower platform.

Carving the cakes to make an inverted triangle shape.

Using buttercream to crumb coat the cakes and make a smooth surface.

Filling and stacking the remaining five layers of cake to create the helmet.

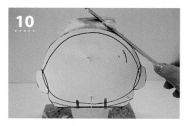

With the template attached, the cake is carved into the rounded shape of the helmet.

The cake carved into the helmet shape, ready for ganaching.

A layer of ganache is applied, smoothed with the flexi smoother and left to set.

6. Add the buttercream filling and the next layers. Carve the cake from the top board to the lower board, creating an inverted triangle shape, and cover with buttercream.

7. Attach the 13cm cake layer to the upper board with ganache and continue to fill and stack the 15cm layers followed by the 13cm and 10cm cakes.

8. Fold the template along the upper board line and attach it to the cake with cocktail sticks. Carve the helmet shape, using the template as a guide.

9. Cover the cake (including the lower section) with ganache and smooth with the flexi smoother. Leave the ganache to set at room temperature.

Covering the Cake

Roll out the white sugar paste large enough to cover the body section and apply it to the cake, folding the paste under the lower board above the legs. Trim off the excess and smooth the seams.

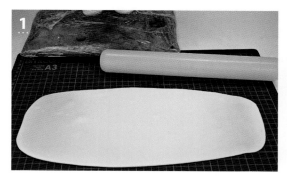

White sugar paste rolled out ready to be applied to the body of the astronaut.

Applying and smoothing the white sugar paste under the lower platform above the legs.

The Arms

1. Roll the two arms using the template to gauge the size and cut the tops at an angle so they sit against the cake. Curve the arms slightly and use the silicone-tipped tool to draw on the crease details.

2. Paint the elbow section with the blue dust and dipping solution and leave it to dry for a few minutes.

3. To make the gloves, take two small balls of black sugar paste and flatten them slightly. Cut a triangle out to make the thumb and fingers section and round it off. Trim the glove so it has a flat edge and stick it onto the arm with edible glue. If you are having trouble getting the glove to stay in place, use a cocktail stick to hold it on.

4. To attach the arms, first work out the position. Push a skewer part way into the arm and remove it, leaving a hole. Push the skewer into the cake leaving a few centimetres exposed and paint it with edible glue. Carefully push the arm onto the skewer, using the hole made previously. Hold the arm in place for a moment and gently release. Repeat on the other side.

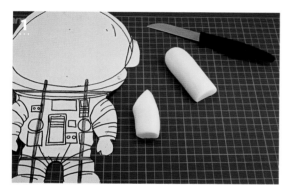

Arms are formed by rolling tubes of sugar paste and cutting at an angle so they will sit flat against the cake.

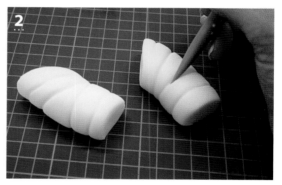

Adding crease details to the arms with the silicone-tipped tool.

Painting blue details onto the elbow section of the arms.

Gloves are made with black sugar paste and attached to the arms with edible glue.

Attaching the arms using skewers and edible glue.

The Helmet

1. Roll out the remaining black sugar paste to cover the front half of the helmet. Trim the excess and smooth the paste with the palm of your hand.

2. Roll a strip of white sugar paste to 5mm in thickness and cut it to 3cm wide. It should be long enough to go all the way around the bottom of the helmet. Brush edible glue around the base of the helmet and attach the strip, being careful to keep it level. Trim the excess and smooth the seam. Use a ruler to lightly mark horizontal a line around the centre of the strip and paint it using the red dust and dipping solution.

3. Cover the back half of the helmet with white sugar paste and carefully trim the excess. Roll out a thick, 5cm-wide strip of sugar paste and

Covering the front half of the helmet in black sugar paste and trimming the excess.

Attaching a strip of white sugar paste around the bottom of the helmet with edible glue.

Painting a red line around the base of the helmet with dust and dipping solution. A faint line is embossed with a ruler as a guide for the paint.

A thick white strip covers the join line between the white and black sections of the helmet and acts as the edge of the visor.

The excess is neatly trimmed off the visor strip.

Clingfilm placed over the sugar paste before cutting gives the circle a domed edge.

A tringle added in each corner of the visor give the helmet a more rounded look.

apply it to the centre of the helmet, where the black and white meet. Trim the end neatly using a dab of glue if needed.

4. Roll out the remaining white sugar paste and cover it with a layer of clingfilm. Cut two circles through the sugar paste with a 5cm circle cutter. This gives the circles a slightly rounded appearance. Attach the circles to the sides of the helmet.

5. Cut two small triangles of sugar paste and attach them to the corners of the helmet on top of the black paste, to give the helmet a more rounded appearance at the front.

Finishing Touches

1. To give the illusion of reflecting light, paint a thin strip of white across the top of the helmet on the right side. Slightly lower down on the left side, paint a white circle with a smaller circle below it.

2. With the remaining sugar paste, make various buttons and switches for the front of the suit. Paint them with the dust and dipping solution and attach to the cake with edible glue. Steam the cake to seal the dust colourings.

3. Remove the clingfilm from the baseboard and add ribbon to the edge with non-toxic glue.

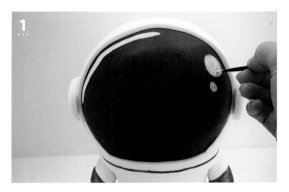

Reflections of light are painted in white on the font of the helmet.

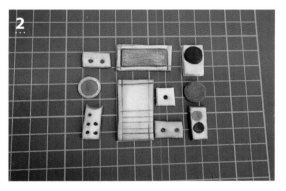

Buttons and dials of various shapes and sizes are cut out of sugar paste and painted with dusts to add interest to the front of the spacesuit.

The buttons are attached with edible glue before the cake is streamed to seal in the dust colour.

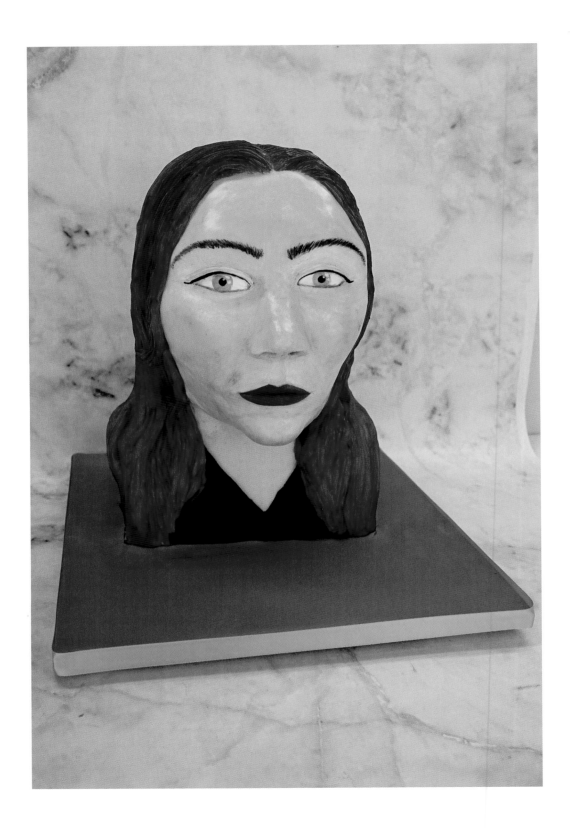

CHAPTER 11

PROJECT 6: BUST STRUCTURE

. . . .

The next project is a bust cake, which is a cake of just a character's head and shoulders. A bust cake can be adapted to be any character or even an animal. The structure remains the same no matter the subject.

For this cake, I used my own face as a guide – the best piece of equipment you can use for a bust cake is a mirror. Practise sculpting noses, lips,

and eyes with sugar paste or modelling chocolate. I have included a basic template for this cake, but you can try printing your own and making a cake of yourself.

This project introduces modelling chocolate. This is perfect for sculpting and blending as it is incredibly soft to work with but firms up as it cools.

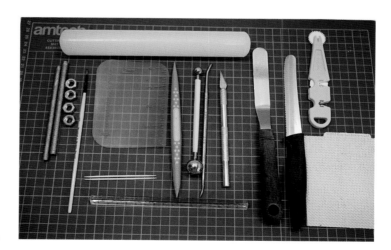

The tools needed for the bust cake.

◀ Project 6: The red lady cake.

Tools and Materials

Tools

- 30cm square MDF board
- Egg-shaped MDF board
- 15cm M8 threaded rod
- M8 washers × 8
- M8 nuts × 8
- Aluminium foil tape
- Furniture feet pads/foam board
- Offset pallet knife
- Smoothing tool
- Flexi smoother
- Craft knife/scalpel
- Serrated knives, large and small
- Ruler
- Rolling pin
- Knitting silicone mould (katysuedesigns. com)
- Fine paintbrush
- Dresden tool or silicone-tipped tool
- Stitching tool
- Ball tool
- Large dusting brush
- Steamer

- 15mm ribbon
- Double-sided tape or non-toxic glue

Extra Equipment

- Drill
- Jeweller's saw
- Vice/clamp
- Coping saw (to cut the MDF board)
- Adjustable spanner

Materials

- Cake (*see* Chapter 5):
    - 20cm × 13cm, 6 layers
    - 20cm × 15cm, 3 layers
- Buttercream, 1 batch
- Ganache, 1 batch
- 2kg white modelling chocolate
- 250g green sugar paste
- Dust colour: red, black, green, white, pink
- Gel colour: ivory, soft caramel, pink
- Dipping solution/alcohol
- Edible glue/glue pen
- Cornflour for dusting

METHOD

Building the Structure

1. Begin by preparing the boards. Cut out the egg-shaped support board and drill a hole in the centre towards the wider end of the board. Next drill a hole in the baseboard in the centre, towards the back edge.

2. Attach the rod to the baseboard using the washers and nuts, and tighten with an adjustable spanner. Cover the egg-shaped board with aluminium foil tape to make it food safe, before securing it the top of the rod. Make sure the board is level and the nuts are threaded tightly.

3. Cover the baseboard, the rod and fittings with the foil tape to make them all food safe.

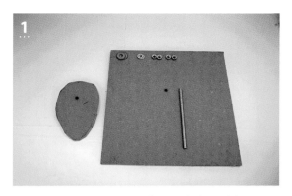

The boards are prepared by drilling the holes and the threaded rod is cut to size.

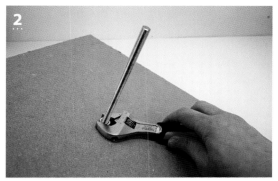

The threaded rod is secured with an adjustable spanner before adding the platform.

Fix the food-safe platform in place and secure it with washers and nuts, ensuring it is level.

The boards and fittings made food safe with aluminium foil tape.

Carving the Cake

1. Spread ganache over the support board and add the first of the smaller cake layers. Continue to fill and stack all six layers, supporting the bottom layer with you hand.
2. Attach the template with cocktail sticks and begin carving the head shape. Round off the back of the head to create an oval shape.
3. Use the small knife to mark in the eye sockets and refine the face shape. Use a mirror to check your own face shape, and gently carve the jaw line and cheek bones.
4. Fill and stack the three larger cake layers on the baseboard under the head. If you are left with a small gap between the lower cake layers and the upper board, make some cake clay to fill the space.
5. Create the shoulders by trimming the top corners from the cake at a 45-degree angle. Carve from halfway under the head down to the board at the same angle to make the chest. Round off the back of the shoulders and neck, giving the back a slight curve in the centre. Check the cake from all angles, making any adjustment to the shape if needed.

The cake filled and stacked on the platform ready to carve. Support the cake with your hand so the corner does not sink.

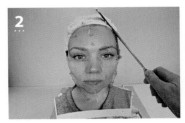

With the template attached to the cake with cocktail sticks, start carving the shape of the head, using the template as a guide.

The back of the cake is rounded into an oval shape.

Carving the eye sockets with a small serrated knife.

Refining the face shape, adding cheekbones.

The remaining cake is filled and stacked on the baseboard.

Cake clay is used to fill the space between the cake and the platform board.

The shoulders are carved by holding the knife at a 45-degree angle and trimming the corners.

Carving the chest area, starting from halfway under the jaw and going down to the baseboard.

Carving the back of the shoulders and the neck.

Rounding off the shoulders to create a curve at the back.

Checking the carved cake from all angles and making refinements if needed.

Covering the Head

1. Apply a layer of ganache and smooth with the flexi smoother. For hard-to-reach places such as the eye sockets, smooth the ganache using your hands. Chill the cake to set the ganache or leave it at room temperature for around half an hour or until it is firm.

2. Roll out the modelling chocolate to 3mm in thickness and brush the ganache with a little water. Cover the head with the chocolate, smoothing it with your hands. Blend the seams using the side of a silicone tool and around the edges under the neck.

A layer of ganache is applied to provide a smooth base and add stability.

Use a flexi smoother to smooth the ganache – or your fingers in hard-to-reach areas.

Cover the face in modelling chocolate and smooth it down with the palm of the hand.

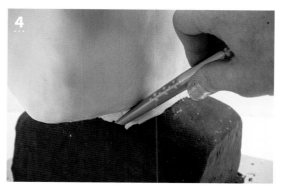

The seams are blended with the side of the silicone-tipped tool, rounding off the jawline.

Forming the Facial Features

1. Take a small ball of modelling chocolate, flatten it slightly and smooth it onto the bottom of the face to create the chin. Use the silicone tool to sculpt the shape, using the mirror and your own chin as a guide. Add a strip of chocolate above the chin to create the lip area and blend the seams.

2. Place a triangle of chocolate for the nose and sculpt the shape. Trim excess chocolate away with a craft knife or add more chocolate as needed. Take your time and look at the

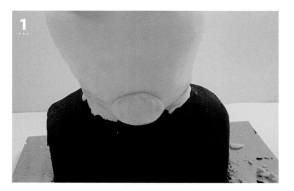

The chin is created by adding a small ball of modelling chocolate and sculpting the shape.

A strip of chocolate is added above the chin to build up the mouth area.

contours of your own nose. Smooth the area with a Dresden or silicone tool. Carve out the nostril with the Dresden tool. It is best to start small and make the nostrils larger gradually, checking the shape in the mirror. Finally, use the silicone-tipped tool to indent around the outside of the nostrils to define the shape.

3. Using the ball tool, add an indent under the nose to form the philtrum. Mark in the position of the mouth and blend in a strip of chocolate to make the top lip. Using a flat-edged silicone tool, gently pull the lip upwards, giving it a slight curve and creating the shape. Use the side of the tool to shape the bottom lip. Draw on the nasolabial folds (smile lines) and smooth the edges.

4. Next create the brow bone by adding modelling chocolate above the eye sockets and blending it in. Have a look at your own brow and see how prominent it is. Mark the edges of the eyes and apply two small strips of chocolate to form the upper eyelids. Place an almond-shaped ball in each eye socket and smooth it under the eyelid, forming the shape of the eye. Add chocolate to the lower lid area and blend, using the silicone-tipped tool to sculpt the shape. Add a few fine lines around the eyes and cheeks.

Overheating

Be wary of hot hands that can make the modelling chocolate oily and too soft to work with. If this happens, leave the chocolate to rest for a few minutes and run your hands under the cold water tap to cool them down.

The nose shape is formed by adding a triangle of modelling chocolate. The chocolate is smoothed and sculpted with a silicone tool.

Sculpting the nose using a Dresden tool.

Marking and carving out the nostrils. It is better to start smaller than you need and adjust the shape as you go.

Refining the shape of the nostrils with a silicone tool.

Defining the outside of the nostril area with the silicone-tipped tool.

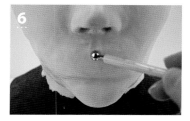

Creating the philtrum by drawing a channel with the small ball tool.

Marking in the mouth before adding the lips.

Creating the top lip by adding a strip of modelling chocolate and blending it into the philtrum.

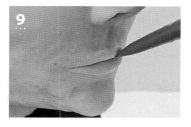

Forming the shape of the top lip by gently pulling a flat silicone tool up, creating a curve.

Shaping the bottom lip.

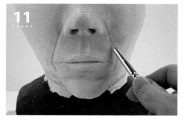

Drawing in the smile lines with the silicone-tipped tool. Round the edges to create a natural look.

Adding modelling chocolate above the eyes for the eyebrows.

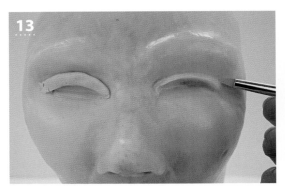

Strips of modelling chocolate are added and blended to the eyes to form the upper eyelids.

Forming the eyes with almond-shaped balls of chocolate.

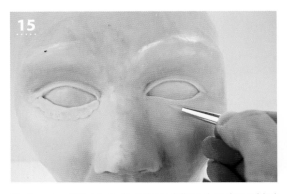

The lower eyelids are made with modelling chocolate added under the eyes.

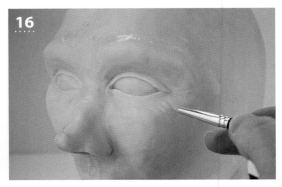

Fine lines are added around the eyes and cheeks.

Covering the Torso

1. Roll out the modelling chocolate to cover the neck and shoulders. Trim the excess and smooth the seams. Make the neckline with two strips of modelling chocolate added in a V shape.

2. Dust the knitting mould with cornflour to prevent it from sticking and press it into the neckline to create a fabric effect. Continue pressing the mould all over the jumper and finish the neckline with the stitching tool.

The neck, chest and shoulders are covered with modelling chocolate and a neckline is added to the jumper.

Embossing a knitted texture onto the jumper to create interest.

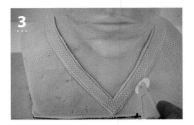

Adding a stitching effect to fabrics gives a realistic look.

Adding the Hair

1. Use long, thick strips of modelling chocolate to build up the hair, adding texture with the silicone tool. For the hair line, lightly drag the chocolate down onto the forehead to create a hair effect.

2. Why not try a different hairstyle? Create curls by wrapping strips of chocolate around a tool handle or try a pony tail. You may need to add ears if they would show.

Thick strips of modelling chocolate are added to the head to create hair.

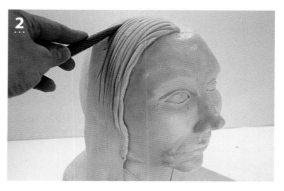

Texture is added to the hair with the silicone tool. Drawing lines of varying depth gives the hair volume.

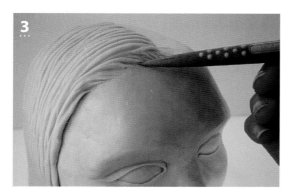

Creating the hairline by gently pulling the chocolate onto the forehead and blending.

More modelling chocolate is added to create a full head of hair.

Adding Colours

1. Dilute a few drops of gel colour with 15–20ml of water to make a translucent paint for the skin. I used soft caramel with a touch of pink. Test the colour on some spare chocolate before applying it to the cake. Paint the face and neck areas with a wide brush. Do not make the chocolate too wet or it will start to bead.

2. Paint the whites of the eyes with dust mixed with dipping solution and leave them to dry for a few minutes before painting the irises. I am using green for the eyes, but you could try another colour. First paint a light green circle and edge it with a darker shade. Add darker lines going inwards and blend them out with some alcohol or dipping solution. Add the black pupils in the centre. Once the pupils are dry, add three white dots to create light reflections.

3. Paint on the eyebrows, using fine, short strokes of brown. Add definition to the eyes with black eyeliner on the top lid. Line the inside of the bottom lids with pink and add a pink dot to the inside corner of each eye to make the tear ducts.

4. Paint the lips and hair with red, and to complete the face, add some pink dust to the cheeks with a large dusting brush. Finally, paint the jumper black, taking care around the hair. Lightly steam the cake to seal the dust colours.

Make up a translucent paint by diluting gel colour with water. Always test the colour on a piece of scrap chocolate before painting on the cake, as the yellow tint of the chocolate can alter the paint colour.

The whites of the eyes are painted with dust colour mixed with dipping solution.

Create some variation to the eye colour by starting with the lightest shade. Outline the eye with a darker shade and add a few lines toward the centre. Blend the colours with dipping solution.

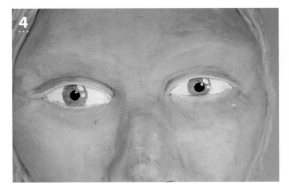

Paint on black circles for the pupils and then add three dots of white to create to recreate the effect of light reflecting in the eyes.

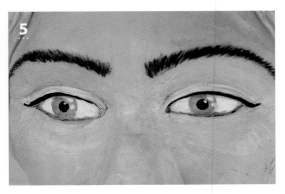

Finish the eyes by adding eyeliner to the top lid and pink to the waterline. A dot of pink in the inner corner of each eye forms tear ducts.

The hair is painted red using dust colour and dipping solution. Use different shades of red to add variation and interest.

A light dusting of pink adds life to the cheeks.

Colouring the jumper with black dust and dipping solution.

Covering the Board

I kept the board simple for this cake, matching the green colour of the eyes. Roll out 250g of green sugar paste and apply to the board in sections, smoothing the seams as you go. Edge the board with ribbon using not-toxic glue.

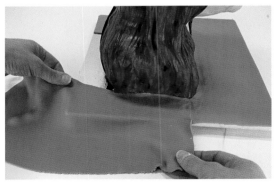

Covering the board with sections of green sugar paste. The seams are blended and smoothed.

CHAPTER 12

PROJECT 7: ARMATURE AND AIRBRUSHING

· · · · · · · · · · · ·

One of my favourite things to carve is a dragon. A fun mix of carving and sculpting brings the dragon to life, and the details make each one different. You can give your dragon character just by changing eye shape or adding teeth. It can be made cute for a young child, or more menacing for an adult or teen. You could add scales and wings, or experiment with opening the mouth and adding a forked tongue.

The dragon cake has a simple structure, with just a dowel to support the neck and armature wire to support the head.

This project introduces the use of the airbrush. An airbrush is great for layering colours, creating graduated colour, and creating depth. Practise controlling the air flow on a piece of paper before airbrushing the cake. The movement should come for the elbow, not the wrist, to avoid patchy colouring.

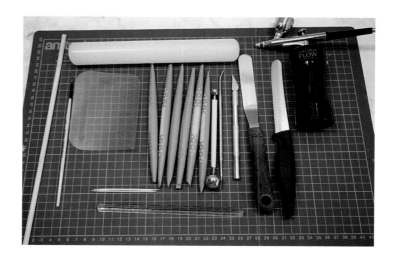

Tools needed to create the dragon cake.

◀ Project 7: The dragon cake.

Tools and Equipment

Tools
- 30cm square MDF board
- 30cm bamboo dowel
- 17 gauge (1.2mm) armature wire
- Aluminium foil tape
- Furniture feet pads/foam board (optional)
- Offset pallet knife
- Smoothing tool
- Craft knife/scalpel
- Serrated knives, large and small
- Flexi smoother
- Wooden skewer
- Airbrush
- Ruler
- Rolling pin
- Fine paintbrush
- Dresden tool
- Silicone-tipped tool (sugar shapers)
- Ball tool
- Steamer
- 15mm ribbon
- Double-sided tape or non-toxic glue

Extra Equipment
- Drill
- Hot-glue gun

Materials
- Cake (*see* Chapter 5):
   - 28cm × 18cm, 3 layers
   - 25cm × 18cm, 1 layer
   - 10cm × 18cm, 1 layer
   - 11.5cm × 10cm, 2 layers
   - 10cm × 10cm, 2 layers
- Buttercream, 1 batch
- Ganache, 1 batch
- 1.5kg white modelling chocolate
- 50g black sugar paste
- 300g grey sugar paste
- Dust colour: red, black, white, yellow, and gold
- 100g caster sugar
- Airbrush colour: yellow, red, brown
- Dipping solution/alcohol
- Edible glue/glue pen
- Cornflour for dusting

METHOD

Preparing the Board and Building the Structure

1. Using the template as a guide, mark the placement of the dowel and drill a hole through the board. Add feet to the underside of the board if required. Sit the dowel in the drilled hole so it is flush with the base of the board. Secure the dowel in place with hot glue and leave it to set. Once the glue is firm and the dowel is secure, cover the board and the glued portion of the dowel with the aluminium foil tape to make it food safe.

2. Measure the armature wire around the shape of the dragon's head on the template and double it. Fold the wire in half and twist it tightly. Create the shape of the head by folding the twisted wire again and attaching it to the dowel. Snip off the excess and wrap the wire around the dowel, securing it with a dab of hot glue. Wrap the wire and glued area with the foil tape, ensuring it is all covered.

Use the template to determine the position of the wooden dowel. Mark and drill the hole.

Securing the dowel with hot glue.

The board and dowel covered with foil tape to make it food safe.

Twisting the armature wire to create a support for the dragon head.

Forming the support for the head with twisted armature wire.

Attaching the wire to the dowel by twisting it in place.

Once twisted into place, the armature wire is secured with a dab of hot glue.

The wire and glue covered with aluminium foil tape to make it food safe.

Carving the Dragon

1. Place the first layer of cake onto the board by making a cut level with the dowel in one of the short sides and sliding it on. Fill and stack the remaining cake in decreasing order of size, with the smaller layers stacked over the dowel to make the neck.

2. Attach the template to the side of the cake with cocktail sticks. You may wish to fold the head section out of the way for now. Begin carving the back section, keeping the knife level so the height is even on both sides. Carve the neck shape, supporting the cake with your hand as you cut. Once ganache is applied, the neck will become more stable.

3. Remove the template and begin carving the front into a pyramid shape. Round off the edges and refine the shape. The cake will begin to resemble a swan.

4. Continue to carve the back section, referring back to the template. A good tip when carving animals (even fantasy ones), is to lightly score

Stack the first layer of cake around the dowel.

The cakes filled with vanilla buttercream and stacked ready to carve.

The template is attached to the cake with cocktail sticks and used as a guide for carving the shape.

The font of the cake is carved into a pyramid shape to begin shaping the neck.

Refining the neck shape and rounding off the edges.

Carving the body shape.

Trimming away the bottom edge of the cake to give a more rounded appearance.

Carving the hips with the small serrated knife.

Refining the neck shape while supporting the cake with the hand.

Check the cake from all sides, making any adjustments if needed.

a line down the centre of the back to mark the creature's spine. Work outwards from the spine, looking from above to carve the sides evenly. Trim around the bottom edge of the cake, holding the knife at a 45-degree angle.

5. Using the template, mark on the back hip and trim away the cake around it with the flat edge of the knife, leaving the hip section wider. Round off the edges of the hip.

6. Supporting the neck with one hand, refine the shape, tapering towards the top where the head will be. Check the shape from all angles, making any adjustments if needed.

Covering the Cake and Sculpting the Head

1. Apply a layer of ganache to the cake and smooth with a flexi smoother. Allow the ganache to set either at room temperature or in the fridge until it is firm. Lightly brush the ganache with water and roll out a large piece of modelling chocolate to cover the body and neck, blending the seams.

2. To form the head, add a ball of modelling chocolate to the foil-wrapped armature wire. Add more chocolate to build up the shape and smooth it onto the neck with the silicone tool. If the chocolate gets too warm and begins to droop, leave it to rest for 5 minutes and cool your hands with cold water. Mark the placement for the nostrils, eyes, and mouth.

3. Using the small end of the ball tool, make two indents for the eyes. Flatten two pea-sized balls of black sugar paste and place them inside the eye sockets, using the ball tool to smooth them down.

4. For each eye, roll a small ball of modelling chocolate to make the eye and place in the eye

The cake is covered with ganache to add stability, and smoothed with a flexi smoother to create a good base for the modelling chocolate.

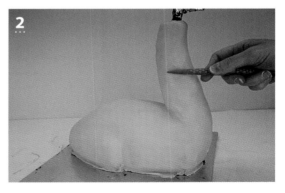

The cake is covered with white modelling chocolate and the seams smoothed.

Beginning to mould the head with modelling chocolate.

Blending the head to the neck so the joins are not visible.

The eyes, nostrils and mouth placements are marked on with the silicone tool.

The ball tool is used to form the eye sockets on the head.

The eye sockets are lined with black sugar paste.

The eye and eyelids are put in place and blended.

Creating the nostrils by gently lifting the silicone tool, forming small mounds.

The jaw and mouth are defined with the silicone-tipped tool.

Details are added to the face to create interest.

Small lines are drawn on using a pointed tool to indicate the lips over teeth.

Scales are created by embossing the modelling chocolate with the flat end of a wooden skewer. A small drinking straw could also be used.

Adding details to the belly with the silicone-tipped tool.

sockets. Add a small strip of chocolate above and below each eye to form the eyelids and blend. To make the nose, push the end of the silicone tool into the chocolate and very gently pull it up, creating the nostril.

5. Define the mouth by gently indenting the chocolate beneath it with the silicone-tipped tool, creating a larger top lip area. Add details to the head, face and lip area.

6. Create scales by gently pushing the end of a skewer on the face and partly down the neck. Draw larger scales over the belly of the dragon and up the front of the neck.

Forming the Limbs and Tail

1. Roll a tube of modelling chocolate to around 13cm long and 4cm thick. Make an indent in the centre with your finger and bend the chocolate into a right angle. Taper the lower section to form the forearm and wrist and attach it to the body. Blend the seams and add some creases.

2. To make each hand, flatten a small ball of chocolate and roll four small strips for the fingers. Attach the fingers and blend the seams. Trim the hand and add it to the wrist. Flatten the ends of the fingers so the claws can be added later.

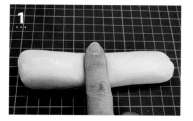

Indenting the chocolate so it can be bent to create the front legs.

Forming the front legs out of modelling chocolate. The forearm section is tapered towards the wrist.

The front legs are attached to the body and the seams blended. Creases and folds are added with the rounded sugar shaper tool.

Forming the hand and fingers with modelling chocolate.

The fingers are attached to the hand and blended to hide the joins.

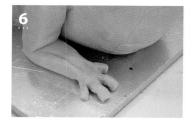

The hand is trimmed and attached to the wrist, and the seams smoothed. The fingers have been flattened to allow for the claws to be added later in the project.

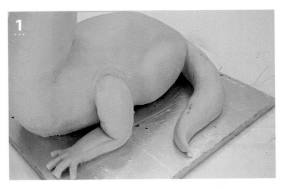

The tail is made with modelling chocolate rolled into a cone shape and slightly flattened at the smallest end.

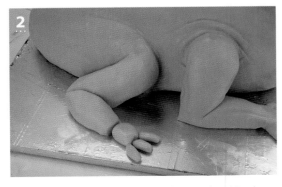

The back legs and hands are put in place ready to blend.

The legs and hands are attached and blended, and the fingers are flattened at the ends ready for the claws.

3. Before making the back legs, the tail needs to be added. Roll the tail into a long, thick cone and slightly flatten it at the smallest end. Smooth the tail onto the body and curve it around the side. Sculpt the back legs and attach them to the base of the hips on each side.

4. Add a leathery texture to the skin by drawing criss-crossed lines with the silicone-tipped tool. Create creases and folds around the base of the neck where it meets the body.

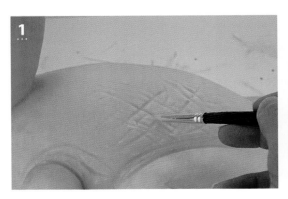

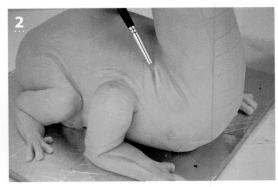

A leathery texture is added all over the skin with the silicone-tipped tool.

Using the Airbrush

1. A large cardboard box makes a perfect spraying booth to protect your surfaces from overspray. If you do not have a box to hand, cover the area in newspaper, including the walls! Place the cake on a turntable in the centre of the spray area.

2. Put yellow airbrush colour into the fluid cup and clip on the lid if your airbrush has one. Wearing gloves if you prefer, very gently pull back the trigger to start the spray. Use large sweeping motions to colour the entire dragon with the yellow. It is best to do several thin layers of colour, so it does not drip.

3. Next add a layer of red to the back and neck of the dragon, leaving the belly and throat yellow. Add a few drops of brown to the cup to make a darker red and very gently spray the creases and folds. Let the colour dry for around half an hour while you clean the airbrush and spray area.

The dragon is airbrushed all over with yellow airbrush colour. Protect the work area with a spray booth or newspaper.

A layer of red is applied to the upper half of the body, neck, and head using the airbrush, leaving the belly and chest yellow.

A few drops of brown are added to the cup to make a darker red, which is gently sprayed in the creases and folds of the body.

The Final Touches

1. Make the 16 claws by rolling small pea-sized balls of black sugar paste between your finger and thumb to make pointed teardrop shapes. Cut the claws to size and attach them to the tips of the fingers, using edible glue if needed. If the airbrush colour is still tacky, this may be sufficient to hold the claws in place.

2. Use the same technique to make spikes with modelling chocolate and place them down the

Claws are made from black sugar paste, by rolling teardrop shapes between the finger and thumb.

The claws are trimmed to size and attached to each of the fingers with a dab of edible glue.

Spikes are made in the same way as the claws and attached to the head, neck, body, down the nose and under the chin.

The spikes are painted with a two-toned effect by layering red dust on top of black dust mixed with dipping solution.

Dry black dust is dabbed abound the snout and eyes.

The nostril cavity is dusted with black to create depth.

back, neck and on the head. Add tiny spikes down the nose and one under the chin.

3. Paint the spikes first with black dust mixed with dipping solution, then paint red dust on the tips. Dab along the snout, around the eyes and inside the nostrils with dry black dust. Steam the dragon to seal the dust colours.

Covering the Board

1. For the board, we are going to create a cobblestone effect. With the grey sugar paste, roll balls of varying sizes and flatten them onto the board in a random pattern. Continue until the entire board is covered, leaving a small border around the dragon.

2. Put 100g of caster sugar in a bowl and add a quarter of a teaspoon of yellow and gold dusts. Mix the dust into the sugar to create sparkling yellow sugar sand. Sprinkle the sand around the dragon, adding gold glitter sprinkles on top (optional).

3. Trim the edges of the board if the grey overhangs, and add a gold ribbon with non-toxic glue.

Grey balls of sugar paste are flattened on the board in a random pattern to create a cobblestone effect.

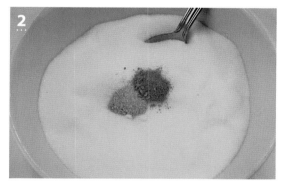

Golden sand is made by mixing yellow and gold dust with caster sugar.

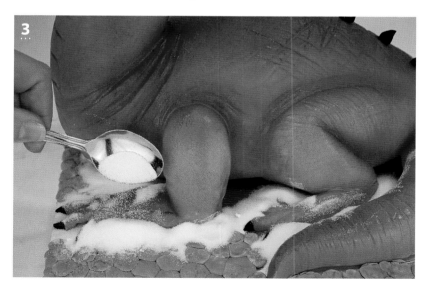

The sugar sand is sprinkled around the dragon to complete the board.

CHAPTER 13

PROJECT 8: THE SHOW STOPPER

• • • • • •

The final cake combines the techniques from the previous projects to make a show-stopping circus elephant. Threaded rods and armature wire are used for the structure, with ganache, modelling chocolate, and sugar paste covering the cake. Rice Krispie treats are introduced to create the balancing ball and the elephant is painted with gel colours and dusts to bring it to life.

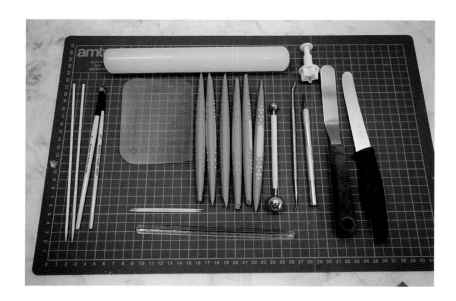

Tools needed to create the elephant cake.

◀ Project 8: The elephant cake.

Tools and Equipment

Tools

- 30cm square MDF board
- 10cm-diameter round MDF board
- 8cm-diameter round MDF board
- 20cm M8 threaded rod, 2 lengths
- 16cm M8 threaded rod
- M8 washers × 12
- M8 nuts × 12
- 85cm 17 gauge (1.2mm) armature wire
- Aluminium foil tape
- Furniture feet pads/foam board
- Offset pallet knife
- Smoothing tool
- Flexi smoother
- Craft knife/scalpel
- Serrated knives, large and small
- Bamboo skewers
- Ruler
- Rolling pin
- Fine paintbrush
- Dresden tool
- Silicone-tipped tool (sugar shapers)
- Star cutters
- Ball tool
- Steamer
- 15mm ribbon
- Double-sided tape or non-toxic glue

Extra Equipment

- Drill
- Jeweller's saw

- Adjustable spanner
- Hot-glue gun
- Airbrush

Materials

- Cake (*see* Chapter 5):
    - 12.5cm-diameter round, 3 layers
    - 14cm-diameter round, 1 layer
    - 10cm-diameter round, 2 layers
    - 7.5cm-diameter round, 1 layer
- Buttercream, 1 batch
- Ganache, 1 batch
- RKT, half a batch
- 5cm poly-ball
- 300g white modelling chocolate
- 50g black sugar paste
- 1kg white sugar paste
- 150g red sugar paste
- 50g blue sugar paste
- Gel colour: pink, yellow, orange
- Dust colour: grey, black, gold, yellow
- 300g white chocolate
- 200g caster sugar
- 100g brown sugar
- Airbrush colour: yellow, red, brown
- Dipping solution/alcohol
- Edible glue/glue pen
- Cornflour for dusting

METHOD

Building the Structure

1. Prepare the three boards and cut the threaded rods to size. Drill two holes, 4cm apart, in the centre of the baseboard. Use these holes as a template to drill the holes in the 10cm support board, adding a third hole in the middle, just above the other two. The small support board has one hole in the centre, and a smaller hole drilled 1cm from the edge. Cover the boards with the aluminium foil and add furniture pads to the underside of the baseboard for feet.

2. Assemble the structure. Attach the 20cm-long rods to the baseboard with the washers and nuts and tighten with the spanner. Next add

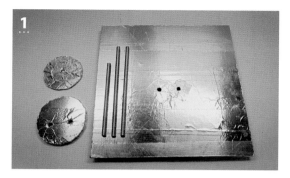

The boards and threaded rods are cut to size ready to assemble the structure.

Building the structure and making it food safe with aluminium foil tape.

the 10cm platform, ensuring it is level. Secure the 16cm rod in the centre hole and add the small platform at the top. Tighten all nuts with the adjustable spanner, ensuring the structure is solid. Cover the rods, nuts and washers with foil tape to make them food safe.

The Ball and Hindlegs

1. Make the RKT according to the recipe in Chapter 5, leaving it to cool for a few minutes so it is not too hot to handle, but still sticky.

Form a 10cm ball on the baseboard around the rods, squeezing the RKT so it holds its shape. If the mixture is too sticky, rub butter or margarine over your hands and the mixture will come away. Once you are happy with the ball shape, leave it to completely cool and set firm.

2. Cover the ball with a layer of ganache and smooth it with the flexi smoother. When it is set, roll out the red sugar paste and cover the ball, smoothing it on with the palm of your hand. Very thinly roll

Forming a large ball of Rice Krispie treats around the threaded rods.

The ball is left to cool and set firm.

A layer of ganache is applied to the ball and smoothed with the flexi smoother.

The ball is covered with red sugar paste and blue stars are added.

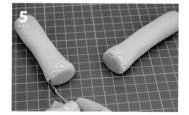

Modelling the legs and feet with grey sugar paste.

Making cuts down the length of the legs allows them to be attached around the threaded rods.

The legs are attached to the top of the ball around the rods.

Grey sugar paste is added under the platform to form the bottom of the body.

out the blue sugar paste, cut several stars, and add them to the ball with some edible glue.

3. Knead together 900g of white sugar paste with 10g of black to make the grey for the elephant. Form the legs by rolling 3cm-thick columns of grey sugar paste and slightly pinch out the feet. Draw four toes on each foot. Make a cut lengthways down the centre of each leg to allow space for the rods. Paint edible glue down each side of the cut.

4. Place the legs on top of the ball, wrapping the sugar paste around the rods. You may need to trim them to fit under the platform. Blend the join seam at the back. Add more grey sugar paste to the underside of the platform to make the curve of the body.

The Body

1. Cover the legs and ball with clingfilm and spread ganache over the lower platform. Stack and fill the 13cm layer, followed by the 14cm layer then the second 13cm layer. Before the final layer is stacked, the armature wire to support the trunk must be added.

The cake is stacked, and armature wire is folded and twisted tightly to support the trunk.

The armature wire is threaded through the drilled hole and secured in place to support the trunk.

The remaining cake is stacked ready to carve.

The body is carved using a large serrated knife.

Ganache is applied and smoothed with the flexi smoother to create an even base.

2. Take the 85cm length of wire, fold it in half and twist it tightly together. Fold it in half a second time and twist it again. Thread one end of the wire through the hole on the side of the platform and twist to secure it. Cover the underside with foil tape and stack the remaining 12.5cm layer.

3. Apply ganache to the upper platform and add the 7.5cm cake. The armature wire will poke through the cake, so add some ganache around the wire to hold it in place.

4. Carve the cake into a teardrop shape, wider towards the middle and tapered at the ends. Apply a layer of ganache and smooth with the flexi smoother.

The Head

1. Fill and stack the two remaining 10cm layers to carve the head. Begin rounding off the top and the bottom edges to make it circular. Trim the forehead area to make it egg-shaped, tapering at the thinnest end.

2. Apply a layer of ganache to the top of the cake and attach the head. Once the ganache has set and the head is firmly in place, gently pull the armature wire away from the head and cover it with foil tape. Bend the wire back up to make the trunk shape and secure it to the front of the head cake with the ganache.

3. Apply a layer of ganache over the head and smooth. Sculpt the elephant's trunk by adding a small amount of modelling chocolate along the wire. Build up the shape with more chocolate and smooth it onto the head. Be careful not to press too hard or the ganache may crack. If this happens, repair the crack with a little more ganache smoothed on with your finger. Leave the end of the armature wire exposed, so the balancing ball can be added later on.

Carving the head with a small knife.

The bottom edge is trimmed to give a rounded appearance.

The cake is carved into an egg shape, tapered towards the trunk area.

The head is attached with a layer of ganache and the armature wire is covered with foil tape to make it food safe.

The wire is held in position with ganache.

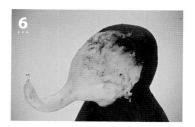
The trunk is sculpted with modelling chocolate.

Covering the Cake and Adding Details

1. Roll out the grey sugar paste and apply it to the cake in sections, beginning with the body, and smooth the join lines. Add grey sugar paste to the top of the legs to create the thighs.

2. With the silicone tool, create a leathery texture over the skin by lightly drawing criss-crossed lines. Continue the texture over the head and draw creases along the trunk.

3. Take a small triangle of grey sugar paste and attach it under the trunk to form the mouth, blending the seams. Draw on the mouth with the silicone tool and use the small ball tool to indent the eyes.

4. To make the ears, roll out the grey sugar paste to a thickness of 1mm. For each ear, cut out the

The body and head covered with grey sugar paste.

Grey sugar paste is added to the top of the legs to crate the thighs.

Texture is added to the skin using the silicone tool.

Adding texture to the trunk and head.

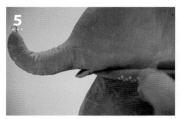

The mouth is added on with sugar paste.

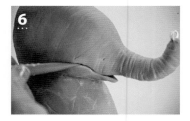

The mouth is drawn on with a silicone tool.

Making indents with the small ball tool to create eye sockets.

Cutting out the ear shapes from the grey sugar paste.

Pea-sized balls of black sugar paste are added to create the eyes.

Strips of sugar paste are attached above and below the eyes to form the eyelids, and blended.

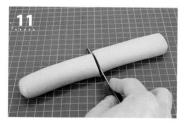

Cutting the sugar paste to make the arms.

Trimming the arms so they have a flat end to attach to the body.

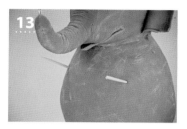

Skewers inserted in place on the body to attach the arms.

Attaching the arms and adding texture with the silicone tool.

Creating folds and creases around the arms and belly area.

ear shape and apply glue along the back side of the longest edge. Attach the ear to the head, folding it forwards. Pinch the edge of the ear with your finger and thumb to create ruffles.

5. Roll two pea-sized balls of black sugar paste and place them in the eye sockets with edible glue. Form the eyelids with two small strips of sugar paste and blend the seams.

6. Roll a column of grey sugar paste around 3cm thick and 20cm long. Cut the column in half to make the front legs. Make an indent a third of the way along each arm so the sugar paste can be bent, and trim the top at an angle so the leg can be attached to the body. Draw four toes on each foot.

7. Decide where to attach the front legs by checking the placement against the body, and insert skewers, making sure they do not go through the back of the body. Paint the skewers with edible glue and gently push on the arms.

8. Add some folds and creases around the front legs and belly area with the silicone tool.

The Finishing Touches

1. Colour a small amount of white sugar paste with the pink gel colour and roll it out to a thickness of 1mm. Using a scallop-edged square cutter, cut a square for the headdress. Attach the square to the elephant's head with some edible glue. Colour some white sugar paste with the yellow gel colour to make gold trim and add some blue balls to embellish the headdress.

2. Put 25ml of water into a ramekin and add half a teaspoon of grey dust colour. Using a wide paint brush, paint the grey dust mixture on the elephant so the colour falls into the creases. While the paint is still wet, use a smaller dusting brush to dab the deeper creases with dry black dust and blend it out using the wet paint already on the body.

3. The final part of the elephant cake is the ball balancing on its trunk. Take a 5cm poly-ball and insert a skewer, like a lollipop.

4. Melt the 300g of white chocolate in the microwave in 30-second blasts until it is smooth and silky. Add a squeeze of orange gel colour and stir well. Take a drinking glass or mug and check the poly-ball fits without touching the sides. Pour the chocolate into the glass and slowly dip the ball in the chocolate. Carefully lift the ball straight up and out so it does not scrape against the side of the glass and remove the chocolate. Hold the ball over the glass until it stops dripping, then turn it upright, holding the skewer. Insert the skewer into a cake dummy and place the chocolate-coated ball into the fridge to set.

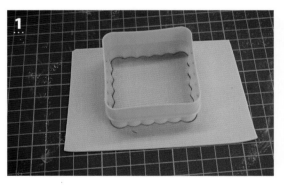

Cutting a scalloped square to make the headdress from pink sugar paste.

Painting the elephant with dust and water to emphasise the skin texture.

The embellished headdress.

Creating shadows under the creases and folds.

Covering the poly-ball with melted white chocolate.

Lift the ball straight up and out of the glass without touching the sides.

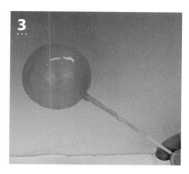

The poly-ball covered with white chocolate.

5. Mix the caster sugar and brown sugar together in a bowl and add half a teaspoon of yellow dust to create sand. Add the ribbon to the edge of the board with non-toxic glue to keep the sand in place. Paint the board with edible glue and sprinkle over the sand, so none of the silver board is visible. Add a few sprinkles and a spray of edible glitter (optional).

6. Remove the chocolate-covered sphere from the fridge and cut the chocolate from the skewer with a craft knife, so the skewer can be removed. Push the ball onto the armature wire at the end on the trunk, supporting the trunk from underneath. Work quickly so the warmth from your fingers does not start to melt the chocolate.

7. Once the ball is securely in place, thinly roll out some blue sugar paste and cut out small stars using a star cutter. Attach the stars to the ball with a dab of edible glue.

Making sugar sand to cover the board.

The board is edged with ribbon and covered with the sugar sand.

Sprinkles and glitter are added to the sand.

Trimming away the chocolate so the skewer can be removed.

The poly-ball is pushed onto the armature wire at the end of the trunk.

Stars are added to the balancing ball.

TEMPLATES

· · · · · · · · ·

Templates are provided here for projects 2 to 8. Scan the templates to your computer or phone and enlarge to the stated size. Print and cut them out, ready to use for the cakes and boards.

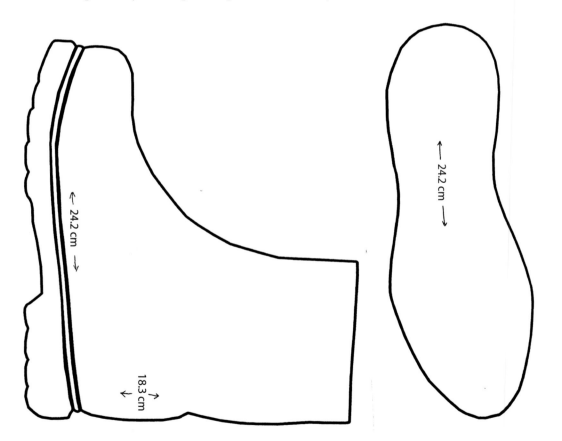

Template for project 2. Enlarge and print the boot at 24.2cm × 18.3cm

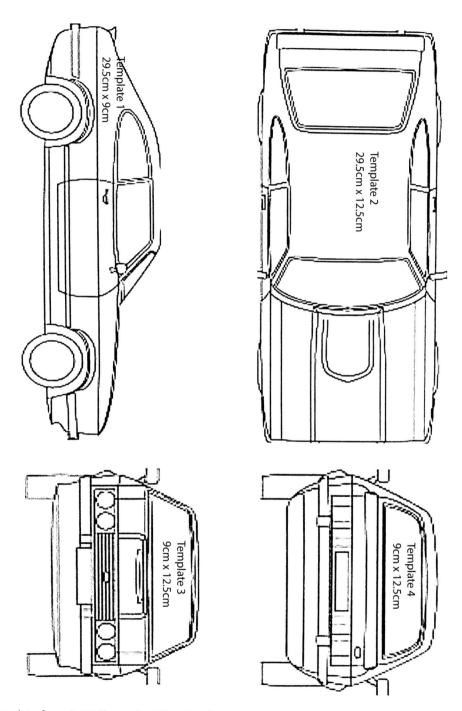

Template 1
29.5cm x 9cm

Template 2
29.5cm x 12.5cm

Template 3
9cm x 12.5cm

Template 4
9cm x 12.5cm

Templates for project 3. The car should be printed 29.5cm × 9cm.

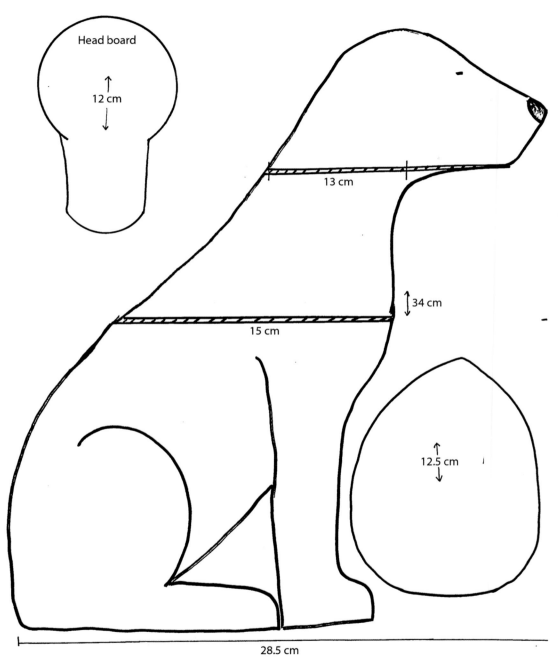

Head board

12 cm

13 cm

34 cm

15 cm

12.5 cm

28.5 cm

Template for project 4. The dog should be 34cm tall.

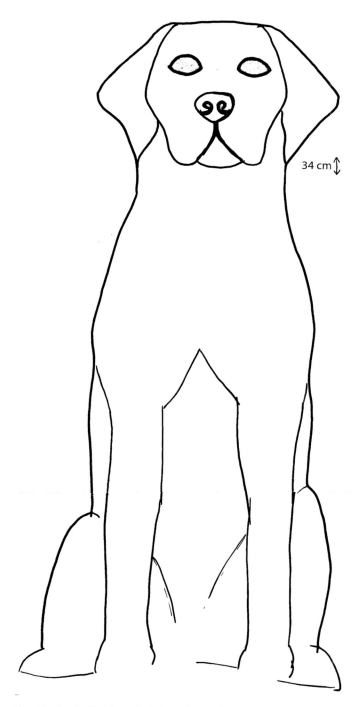

34 cm ↕

The side view for the dog cake. Print at 34cm tall.

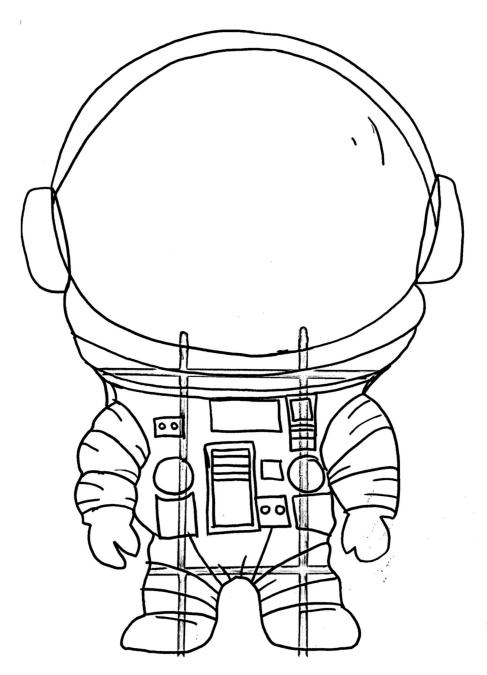

The astronaut cake
template. Print at
29cm tall.

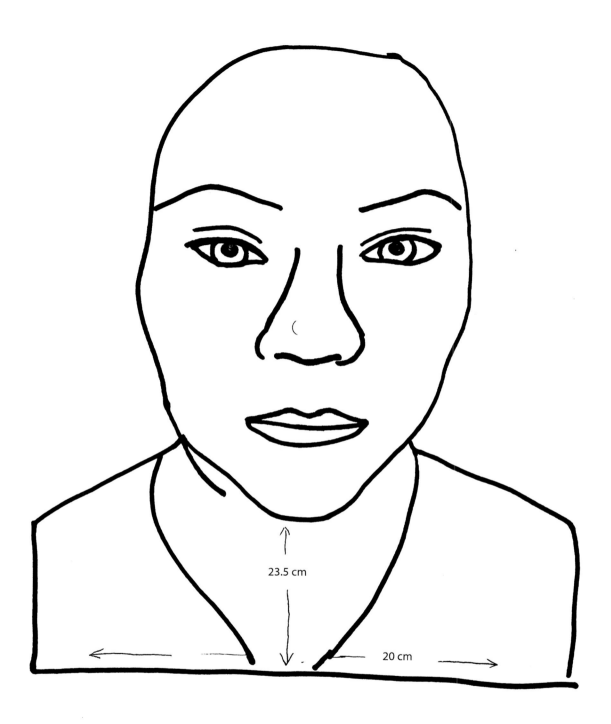

23.5 cm

20 cm

The template for project 6, the bust cake. Print at 23.5cm tall by 20cm wide.

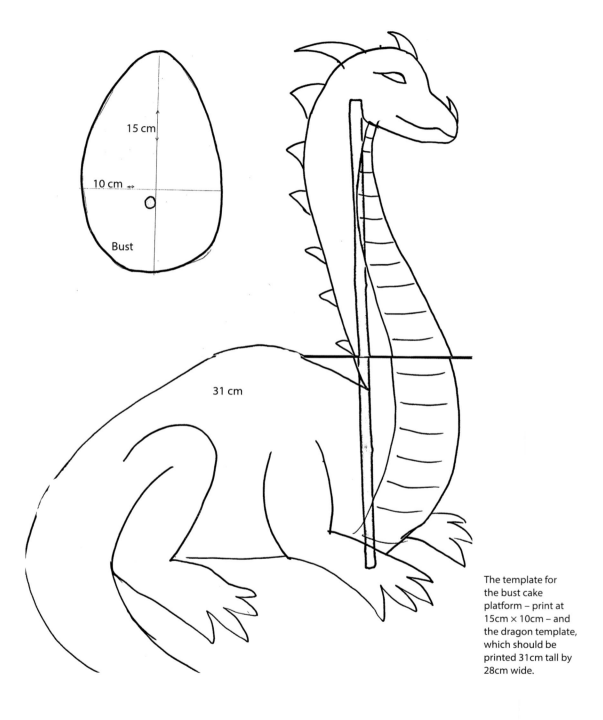

15 cm

10 cm

Bust

31 cm

The template for the bust cake platform – print at 15cm × 10cm – and the dragon template, which should be printed 31cm tall by 28cm wide.

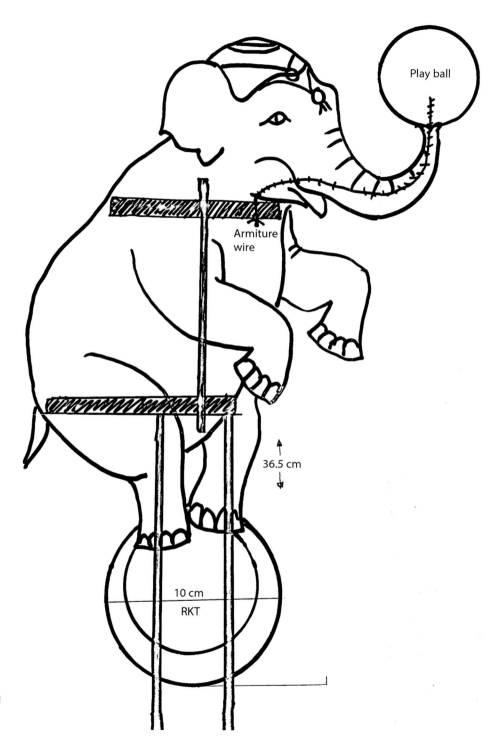

Play ball

Armiture
wire

36.5 cm

10 cm
RKT

The elephant
template should
be printed at
36.5cm tall.

STOCKISTS

· · · · · · · ·

The following UK-based online retailers supply the products used in this book.

Cake Craft Company
www.cakecraftcompany.com

The Cake Decorating Company
www.thecakedecoratingcompany.co.uk

Cake Stuff
www.cake-stuff.com

Dinkydoodle
www.dinkydoodle.co.uk

PME
pmecake.com

Prop Options
www.propoptions.co.uk

Sugar and Crumbs
www.sugarandcrumbs.co.uk

Vanilla Valley
www.thevanillavalley.co.uk

Zoe's Fancy Cakes
zoesfancycakes.co.uk

CONVERSION CHARTS

· ·

Weight

Metric	Imperial
15g	½oz
100g	3½oz
150g	5½oz
200g	7oz
300g	10½oz
400g	14oz
500g	1lb 2oz
600g	1lb 5oz
700g	1lb 9oz
800g	1lb 12oz
1kg	2lb 4oz

Liquids

Quantity	Metric
1tsp	5ml
1tbsp	15ml
¼ cup	60ml
½ cup	125ml
$\frac{1}{3}$ cup	80ml
¾ cup	185ml
1 cup	250ml
1½ cups	375ml
1¾ cups	435ml
2 cups	500ml

Temperatures

Celsius	Fahrenheit	Gas mark
120	250	½
140	275	1
150	300	2
160	325	3
180	350	4
190	375	5
200	400	6
220	425	7
230	450	8
240	475	9

NB these temperatures are given for conventional ovens.

Length

Imperial	Metric
½in	1cm
1in	2.5cm
2in	5cm
3in	7.5cm
4in	10cm
5in	13cm
6in	15cm
7in	18cm
8in	20cm
9in	23cm
10in	25cm
11in	28cm
12in	30cm

Index

· · · · · ·

airbrush 7, 15, 21, 111, 119–20

armature 8, 111–3, 115, 123–4, 126–7, 130–1

baking tins 11–2, 34–5

ball tool 13, 45, 70–1, 74, 81, 84, 92, 104–5, 115–6, 128

baseboard 23–5, 27, 90–1, 93, 97, 100–2, 124–5

batter 11, 19, 33–5

bust 99, 137–8

buttercream 8, 11, 12, 19, 34, 36, 42–3, 51, 53, 66, 68, 78–9, 82, 87, 93, 94, 114

cake 7, 8, 11–5, 17–21, 23–5, 29, 33, 34–6, 38–9, 41–5, 47, 51–5, 57–9, 61, 63–4, 66–71, 73–5, 77, 78–83, 86–7, 89–90, 93–5, 97, 99, 101–3, 108–9, 111–5, 119, 123, 126–8, 130, 135–8, 140, 144

carve 7, 8, 25, 33, 42, 52–3, 64–7, 79–81, 101–2, 111, 113–5, 126–7

chocolate 18–21, 36–9, 51, 54, 103–8, 115, 117, 124, 127, 130–1

cocoa powder 33

colour 15, 18–21, 30, 34–6, 54, 58–9, 61, 70–4, 78, 84, 86–7, 90, 97, 100, 108–9, 111–2, 119–20, 124, 130

cornflour 14–5, 29, 46, 54, 106

cutters 13, 17, 24, 54, 124

dipping solution 20, 71–2, 74, 84–6, 93, 95–7, 108–9, 120–21

dowel 77–8, 83–4, 111–4

drill 24, 27, 90, 100, 112–3, 124

drum 23, 41, 59, 78, 82

dust colours 15, 20, 108, 121

edible glue 21, 54–7, 59, 70–1, 73, 75, 83–7, 93, 95–7, 120, 126, 129–31

equipment 7, 11, 24, 99

ethanol 20

flexi smoother 12, 42, 43, 44, 54, 68, 81, 94, 103, 112, 115, 125–7

foil tape 24, 27, 78, 89–91, 93, 100–1, 112–3, 124–5, 127

fondant see sugar paste

ganache 8, 12, 18, 36–7, 51–2, 54–5, 68, 78, 81–3, 93–4, 101, 103, 113, 115, 123, 125–7

gel colours 19, 123

madeira 33, 35

materials 7, 8, 13, 17

modelling chocolate 8, 13–4, 17–9, 21, 29, 31, 38, 39, 99, 100, 103–7, 112, 115–8, 120, 123–4, 127

modelling tool kit 12

modelling tools 13

moulds 17–8

paintbrush 14, 21, 71, 74, 78, 86, 90, 92, 100, 112, 124

palette knife 12, 54, 68, 78, 81, 90, 100, 112, 124

recipe 33, 36, 125

ribbon 41, 49, 59, 74, 78, 87, 90, 97, 100, 109, 112, 121, 124, 130–1

rolling pin 12, 44

scissors 15, 78

sculpting 7, 13, 17, 24, 99, 104, 111

serrated knife 12, 39, 42, 64–5, 80, 102, 114, 126

silicone 13, 29, 30, 46, 59, 60, 73, 78, 82–5, 90, 93, 95, 100, 103–5, 107, 115–8, 128–9

smoother 12, 30–1, 42, 44, 54, 78, 90, 100, 112, 124

sponge 33–4, 43, 64, 66

stand mixer 11

steamer 15, 20

stitching tool 13, 45–7, 55, 57, 87, 106

sugar paste 8, 12–5, 17–21, 29, 31, 42–7, 49, 51–2, 54–60, 68, 70–5, 78, 81–7, 90, 92–7, 99, 100, 109, 112, 115–6, 120–1, 123–6, 128–31

tape measure 15

templates 7, 8, 15, 51, 64–5, 70, 78, 81, 132

textures 13, 17, 29, 30, 92

threaded rod 27, 90, 100–1, 124

tools 8, 11, 13, 29, 30, 41, 51, 63, 77, 99, 144

turntable 20, 119

wire 8, 13, 24, 30, 111–3, 115, 123–4, 126–7, 131

First published in 2024 by
The Crowood Press Ltd
Ramsbury, Marlborough
Wiltshire SN8 2HR

enquiries@crowood.com

www.crowood.com

British Library Cataloguing-in-Publication Data
A catalogue record for this book is available from the British Library.

ISBN 978 0 7198 4330 3

Typeset by Envisage IT
Cover design by Nick May/www.bluegecko22.com
Printed and bound in India by Thomson Press (India) Ltd

Dedication
For my husband Adam, for always believing in me and my crazy projects.

Acknowledgements
My biggest thank you goes to my family. My husband Adam, for always supporting me and encouraging me in everything I do, even if it's carving a life size dinosaur in our kitchen! Thank you to my amazing children Harry, Dylan, Isaac and Rose, for being patient while I work and eating all of my cake off-cuts. I hope you look at this book in years to come and remember you can achieve your dreams with a little hard work (and not to leave things to the last minute!)

To my dad Terry, for always being there when I need help with a cake structure or to borrow tools and my Mum Angie, for being my biggest cheerleader.

Thank you to my brother in law Dan, for the help with lighting and photography, and to the rest of my family and friends, for putting up with the constant stream of cake photos and cake chatter.

Writing a book has been a dream of mine for many years. I would like to thank the team at Crowood for the amazing opportunity, and to everyone who reads this book.

Happy baking!

RELATED TITLES FROM CROWOOD

· · · · · · · ·

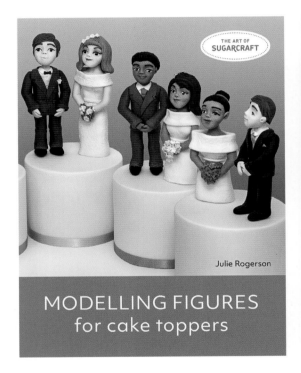

THE ART OF SUGARCRAFT

Julie Rogerson

MODELLING FIGURES
for cake toppers

THE ART OF SUGARCRAFT

CREATING FLOWERS
from flowerpaste

Colette Laura May